MY WORLD IS
GROWING
LARGER

For Louise,
What a treasure
you are. May
we meet again
this life. If not —
Heaven is better
by far!
Psalms 34:1-3
Ruth & Clent
Peterman

MY WORLD IS GROWING LARGER

by Ruth Peterman

TYNDALE
HOUSE
PUBLISHERS
Incorporated

Wheaton
Illinois

Several chapters of *My World Is Growing Larger* appeared originally in periodicals. Tyndale House gratefully acknowledges permission to adapt and reprint these articles:

"Going Down Devil's Hill," "The Old Oaken Rocker," and "The Boy with the Arm" are reprinted by permission of *Scope* (Official Journal of the American Lutheran Church Women), Augsburg Publishing House.

"The Boy with the Arm" was originally published by *Fellowship* magazine, © 1965, used by permission of Scripture Press.

To Grace

Contents

Christmas, 1931

With today's programs for the poor, I often wonder if anybody lives the way we did during the dry years on the farm before Franklin D. Roosevelt initiated the Works Progress Administration.

An article in the *Minneapolis Star* in December, 1973, told of a woman who, with her three children, would have no Christmas because her income was only $370 a month. In 1973 inflation hadn't brought prices to the crazy heights they are today. I wondered how her $370 compared with my father's $40 from WPA in the mid thirties.

The woman told the reporter there would be no presents and no tree. It would be just another day in the year for her and her children.

That trimmings would be few, I could understand. But to have nothing? My mother saved nickels for months before Christmas and after Christmas she started hiding coins for our Fourth of July when we'd either go to Haveman's Grove and celebrate with our Dutch community, or stay at home and eat the goodies she had selected.

Today an overripe banana reminds me of Mother's trunk in her bedroom, where she kept the fruit and candy she had bought the Saturday before our celebration. How Mother managed to save a coin here and there I can now understand. She just never bought anything for herself. Grandma did the mending, and when the patches on the patches wore out on the knees and seats of our long underwear and John's overalls, Mother usually had saved enough from the eggs and cream money to buy a new pair. But she rarely bought anything for herself.

We got into the spirit of Christmas early. We children all had parts in at least two programs—school and church. We memorized all our lines. No one went on stage reading anything, although the teacher prompted from the wings when necessary.

One year I had new shoes of which I was very proud, but in my nervousness I marched onto the platform with my overshoes on. After the program at Hull Church, every child received a lunch bag of candy and nuts and an apple. I always opened my bag to make sure they had remembered to include the chocolate drop. If I was lucky, there might even be two! There it was! I wouldn't eat it right away. I'd save it and relish the longing for it, knowing it was there. I'd suck my hard candies and eat my apple and some peanuts.

Once I offered my only sister, Bessie, four years older than I, something from my bag, and she brought out the chocolate drop. I almost fainted. Laughingly, she put it back and took a red and white peppermint-flavored piece I could spare.

Our school program at Harding No. 4 was an occasion unmatched by any other in our lives. A country school, one room for eight grades, it was heated by a huge round stove protected by a metal jacket to prevent burns. That stove provided excitement today's children will never know. Several times, the pipes fell down and the smoke billowed into the classroom, darkening the high ceiling and walls for years.

I marvel now at the young women teachers' ability to cope. How did they keep the place from burning down? How did they get the pipes back up when they were so hot? Fortunately, each year there would be some fifteen- or sixteen-year-old boys, standing inches taller than our teachers, who returned to eighth grade in the winter to try to get a diploma. (Farm boys often left the classroom for the fields in March to help put in crops, and therefore they had failed their examinations earlier.)

One time we decided to heat our art supplies, including cans of paint. No one thought to remove the covers. That day one loud POP was immediately followed by another, after which we had a technicolored stove.

I skipped second grade because I would have been alone and my teacher thought I'd get along all right with the third graders. I did, but have never learned to print.

My third and fourth grade teacher was of German and French parentage. She had thick black hair set in a permanent wave. She had huge, soft brown eyes and a fair complexion, and was generous with her smiles. I loved her. I don't recall any severe punishments, yet her discipline was good. She wore a different dress every day for several weeks and carried cakes with thick frosting in her lunch box. But when winter set in and her janitorial duties became heavy, she put on a black skirt and sweater which she wore until the middle of March. We girls had all been telling our mothers about our beautiful teacher and her lovely clothes. By the middle of December we were worrying that she'd wear that plain black outfit for the program.

The last week before the program we would have

classes for about two hours. Then our teacher would say, "Push back the desks," and we would rehearse for the program.

The night arrived. All our parents crowded into that little building lit by kerosene lanterns. And that year our teacher had bought a tree! We students had made the decorations—colorful paper chains and strings of popcorn. There was no fire department to place restrictions on the country school, and apparently no parents objected, so we had a heavily decorated tree lit by candles. This was the first Christmas tree I'd ever seen, and I was seven years old.

The program began after a nervous welcome from our teacher. She was dressed in a gorgeous dress I'd never seen before—red with sleeves made of some delicate, sheer fabric.

The upper grades gave a play about a mother who had expressed the wish for slippers for Christmas. Oh, the delicious suspense and excitement each member of the family had, hiding his gift from Mother. And then in the end all of them gave her slippers! I relished it all the more for having been in on the secret.

My turn came to give a recitation. It wasn't meant to be funny, but everybody was laughing. The joke was that I'd learned it from my darling teacher in the exact way she said it—with a German brogue as thick as that of Lawrence Welk, who was then still playing for dances in the Midwest. That whole winter, whenever Hollanders visited each other in our home or theirs, I was asked to say my recitation for their amusement. We didn't realize it until years later, but we Hollanders had our own way of speaking, in direct translations from the Holland or Dutch idiom, that set us apart, too. But in those days we felt quite superior.

The final act of that program was a surprise to me. Santa Claus came onto the stage with a bag full of presents. We didn't allow Santa in our home. My parents considered him a usurper of Christ's honor and banned him forever from our Calvinist chimney. I had therefore applied evangelistic zeal to persuade my friend Dorothy Peterman that there was no Santa Claus. But she asked her mother, who assured her there was indeed a Santa Claus. Dorothy chose to believe her mother.

I enjoyed a forbidden delight in seeing the man himself in costume. "He" also had a pronounced German brogue, and we soon recognized him as Julia, one of our eighth grade girls. Santa distributed the presents we had drawn names for, then gifts from our teacher, and a bag of candy for each of us. Then he "Ho! Ho!'d" a few times, tickled a baby in the front row who began to cry, and disappeared behind the curtain.

After the applause and cheers, our pretty teacher blew out the candles on the tree before all the chairs were pushed back and people went home. I opened my gift from my teacher—a pencil box. In it were two pencils, a six-inch ruler, four crayons (no pink), an eraser, a few pen points and a pen to stick them in, and a half-moon metal thing I had no use for. I used an ink bottle to make circles.

Not all our teachers brought a tree to the school or arranged for Santa to come, but we always had a program well worth waiting for all year.

Letter to the Editor

I felt that article in the paper about the family who would have no Christmas deserved an answer. So I sent off a letter to the editor:

Mrs. Raymond and others will have a slim Christmas. But I hope it will not be "just another day."

We lived in North Dakota in the dry thirties. Little or no cash came into our farm home. It was next to impossible to raise anything. One year the grasshoppers came in a cloud like an Exodus plague and stripped the garden, even eating onions out of the ground.

We ate no butter and few eggs. We had to sell our cream and eggs to get flour with which to bake bread. The bread was often doughy, as the kitchen range didn't work too well.

When we moved to town, we kept our cow. When we had to sell Lucy, we did without milk for a winter. Mother was sickly; I can still picture my father (now in heaven), pouring hot water over our cornflakes before school. Our lunches consisted of bread with such spreads as lard with salt and pepper, or chopped onions.

We never had meat, and for a year or more Mother fried foods in suet. We bought this cow fat in such quantities that the butcher thought we made soap. Mother daily provided a tasty dish of American fried potatoes, always with onions. We learned to eat very fast, as suet congeals when it gets cold. Our palates, as well as our plates, became coated with suet.

Every one of these meager meals was received with thanksgiving.

All year, Mother saved for two occasions: Christmas and the Fourth of July. On Christmas we had candy, peanuts, and, most marvelous of all, a few oranges. We each had a gift. I shall never forget the year I got a ten-cent ring with a red oval stone.

One year Mother must have had a little more money—probably after the government started the WPA. She was able to buy me a set of play dishes which I'd wanted for years. But it was too late. I'd outgrown the desire for a set of dishes. Today it stands, complete, in my buffet—a tribute to parents who paid their doctor bills a dime at a time, gave pennies in church when that was all they had, and saved all year for Christmas.

I hope Mrs. Raymond will read her children the Christmas story and give them each a little present. Christmas programs and church services are free. If she'll take her family to church and make something special for dinner, they will always remember it. Someday they may even write a letter to an editor and tell what their mother accomplished with little.

Christmas just another day? When God so loved that he gave his only Son? When Christ so loved that he left heaven to take the form of a child, only to grow up and die for us? This gift is for all who will receive it—rich or poor.

Father, help us all to be more thankful—to complain less and to make the most of what we have. Help us to receive your gifts with thanksgiving. And may we never, under any circumstances, forget that Christmas is special because you gave your best. Amen.

Beth

Your name suits you, Beth. It speaks to me of gentleness and love.

I'm so glad I met you. I carry in my mind a picture of a little face, usually smiling, sometimes soberly observing.

It worried me that you sat so close to your color television, but your parents didn't seem to feel it would make your vision any worse.

Watching you eat was an experience I shall never forget. Your lip right up to the plate, you literally "shoved" it in. I don't know, Beth, where you put all those baked beans. It seemed you didn't have a signal in your tiny system that flashed "full." Once again, with both of your parents at the table, I needn't have worried.

You quit several times and cheerfully accepted the thorough cleaning up from your mother. But each time you walked past the beans and Jello still on your plate, you stopped to push in a few more tomatoey mouthfuls, soiling your whole face again. When you had finally finished, you crawled up onto your mother's lap. My what a sticky loving you gave her! You just couldn't stop kissing and hugging her. Then you jumped down and brought her your coat. She helped you dress warmly and you ran for the door. But you soon returned to plant still one more kiss on your dear mother's cheek. What a love affair!

You played in the farmyard for quite some time. Occasionally, your mother would check on you, fearing you might have gone to the road. Only once did she find you there; every other time you were "feeding the chickens."

After an hour you came in. You turned on the television and immediately left it. Quietly, your mother urged you to turn it off. "We don't want it on, Beth," she said. You smiled your sweet little smile, but made no move toward the TV. Your mother shut it off and you didn't object.

You soon wearied of the indoors and handed your mother your coat again. She got you ready to play outdoors three times while we visited that afternoon. One time when you came in I showed your mother that you were walking about in her pretty living room with your jeans full of mud. Unruffled, she replied, "She'll just go back out and sit in some more mud anyway." I sometimes think she knew she wouldn't always have you.

Your jeans kept sliding down. "She hasn't any hips," your mother explained. We laughed and wished we had your problem.

You'll never read this, Beth. When you came into this world there were those who wondered why your parents didn't put you in an institution. "She'll forget you in three days," one woman said, not meaning to be cruel. Years later, your mother told me they never considered an institution. Instead, they prayed for strength to care for you and trusted your, and their, heavenly Father to provide for you as long as you would require care.

As I sat at the table with you and your parents and other guests, I marveled at both of your parents. That patience you take so for granted, Beth, most normal children never see in either of their parents. Does God give special qualifications to parents who have extra burdens? I believe he does. But how many parents have the faith to claim those qualifications? More choose the quick abortion or the institution,

9

or, if they keep the Down's syndrome child, miss the blessing with the burden.

It seems now you were a visitor from heaven. You lived with your family near Westfield, North Dakota, for only twelve years and three months. A letter from your mother describes your last day. "She had a restless night. The next morning, she wanted oatmeal for breakfast. I made some but she ate very little. About 11:00 she seemed quite sick, so I took her to the doctor in Linton. Eddie was in the field, so I stopped and told him we were going. Beth sat up and looked out the window. I helped Beth walk to the hospital, but as we reached the door she sank to the floor. An aide brought a wheelchair.

"After X-rays, the doctor said she had double pneumonia, which she'd had several times before. I expected she'd soon be feeling better, as she was getting oxygen and medication. About 5:00 the doctor said he felt she should be transferred to Bismarck to the intensive care unit. He'd done all he could. I thought she was breathing easier and looking better, but he said maybe she would have a turn for the worse during the night and it would be hard to get help. So I telephoned Eddie and told him to come as quickly as he could. By the time he got there Beth had passed away. She died quietly about 6:25 that afternoon."

One often hears the comment that it's not fair to the other children to bring a retarded child into the home—as though God didn't know what he was doing in such cases. In contrast, Alice and Eddie Van Beek and their children demonstrated true family love in their acceptance of little Beth.

Her sisters wrote a memorial obituary which was read at the funeral. "Beth was indeed a 'special' little girl to all who loved her. She had special needs and special problems, but she also brought special blessings. She was always ready with a smile, a hug, or a handshake. Beth may not have been able to learn a lot, but she was a good teacher. She taught many lessons in patience, kindness, and love.

"Sunday was always a big day for Beth, as she loved to go to church and Sunday school. She especially enjoyed the singing. In her own way she loved Jesus, and she now has a new home with him. It's a comfort to know she's now worshiping God with a perfect mind and a beautiful voice."

Dear little Beth, I hope they have baked beans in heaven.

The Premiere

It had been two years since Eunice Kronholm and I had coauthored the story of her kidnapping *(Held for Ransom,* Tyndale House Publishers). The book had been filmed by Ken Anderson, of Winona Lake, Indiana, and tonight the premiere showing was to be held at Northwestern College in Roseville, Minnesota.

One of the bonuses of writing someone's book is meeting the people who played a significant role in the story. One was Pastor Bob McKuen.

In the book, we told of this Episcopal priest going to Gunnar Kronholm's bank to call on Gunnar after seeing him at a Rotary Club luncheon. He remarked that Gunnar seemed depressed and asked if there was anything he could do for him. "Could I pray for you?"

This gave Gunnar a chance to tell why he was feeling so low. A television station was running a series of interviews with one of the kidnappers. The questions asked appeared to be making a case for the defense. The Kronholms' reputations were being destroyed; the FBI had come three times to audit Gunnar's bank.

Gunnar answered the priest, "Yes, I would like you to pray for me."

When I met Bob McKuen the night of the premiere, he told me, "You said in the book that I placed both my hands on Gunnar's head when I prayed."

"You did. That's what Gunnar told me."

"I didn't put my hands on his head."

Seeing my amazement, he continued. "I wanted to put my hands on his head, but I didn't. I held back. I knew God wanted me to, but I refrained. God put my hands on Gunnar's head. He felt my hands even though they were folded in front of me."

Together we marveled at the ways of God.

Whose head would you like God to put your hands on today?

O the depth of the riches both of the wisdom and knowledge of God! how unsearchable are his judgments, and his ways past finding out! (Romans 11:33).

Father, what a wonderful God you are! If any of my children need comfort today, Lord, will you place my hands on their heads for me, please? Thank you.

The Gift of Prayer

The night of the premiere of "Held for Ransom" I also met Irene Gifford. Known for her gift of prayer, Irene had prayed with Eunice and Gunnar Kronholm several times during the trying days following Eunice's release.

Late one night, two months after Eunice had escaped, Gunnar had discovered a man in the crawl space under their house. Standing on the trap door with a loaded shotgun, Gunnar kept the man down there until the police arrived.

The police sent the Kronholms to the neighbors. The man in the crawl space remained so silent that the police began to doubt whether Gunnar had really seen someone. When they went down under the house to investigate, the man held his gun on them and got away. The next day he was caught in the woods following a shootout with the FBI.

When their home was invaded, the Kronholms lost all their security. Even after doing everything Eunice's doctor recommended, they were afraid. They kept guns under every bed; Gunnar's bank installed a security system in their house; Gunnar arranged to have a college student live with them for the summer so Eunice wouldn't be alone all day; they both took valium as needed.

They lived day and night in fear. Gunnar's nightmares consisted of fighting off a kidnapper. Eunice's mind went steadily back to her kidnapping—the details of how she had been grabbed early one morning as she was getting into her car. On one of the worst of these nights Eunice called Irene Gifford at midnight.

Irene prayed with Eunice and Gunnar over the telephone. That night they both rested well.

Two years later, I met Irene. Rather apologetically I said, "I hope you didn't mind the version of the prayer I recorded in the book. Eunice thought it was quite a bit like yours, but she didn't remember exactly." Embarrassed, I rushed on, "I certainly don't have the gift of prayer."

Instantly, the Holy Spirit rebuked me.

The little woman with the short straight brown hair smiled generously. "It was quite all right."

I began to think of the many times I'd interceded for others. I thought of how often my husband's burdens were lightened after I'd prayed. I remembered the times I'd prayed with friends and they had sensed answers even before they came. The Holy Spirit reminded me of innumerable times I'd asked for even small things—like the time I went shopping for a white purse and was led to one for the exact amount of the check I'd received from Nella and Rick for my birthday.

Shortly after meeting Irene, I prayed over the telephone with three different persons in one week. One was a staunch Catholic, reared in the old tradition, who had a recurrence of cancer. Another was a Jewish girl who had lost her job and was being slandered. A third was a mother whose ex-husband was asking the court, three years after the divorce, for two of their five children. In each case we let our requests be made known unto God, and prayed for his holy will. Each of these people experienced a great lifting of their burdens as we prayed. I felt such a filling of the Holy Spirit, and such gratitude that I could pray with these people, that I walked around the house weeping with joy. Later all of them wrote or called me to repeat their thanks for my sharing their load and carrying it to Jesus.

Never again will I consider prayer a gift of the few. As a songwriter has expressed it, prayer is the soul's sincere desire, uttered or unexpressed. It's not the one who prays but the One who is prayed to who has the power!

If ye abide in me, and my words abide in you, ye shall ask what ye will, and it shall be done unto you (John 15:7, KJV).
But if you stay in me and obey my commands, you may ask any request you like, and it will be granted! (John 15:7, TLB).

Lord, just as Moses stepped into the breach between you and your people, you give us the privilege of interceding for others. May we abide in and obey you, that you may grant our requests. Amen.

Has Your Water Been Turned to Wine?

In his commentary on the story of Jesus' first miracle, when he turned the water into wine, Matthew Henry asks, "Has your water been turned to wine?"

Jesus had been invited to a wedding, very likely the wedding of a relative, since his mother Mary was there. Jesus' disciples were also invited. Perhaps more people came to the wedding than had been invited. At any rate, the supply of wine ran out. Jesus' mother informed her son of the need: "They have no wine."

His answer, "Woman, what have I to do with thee? Mine hour is not yet come," implied that he hadn't planned to work a miracle this early in his ministry. However, because of the need, he did.

Mary appeared unoffended at being called "Woman," and going back to the servants she said, "Do whatever he tells you."

Every home in the East had waterpots standing near the door, where people could wash after traveling and do their ceremonial cleansing. These weren't gold-lined vessels. They were just plain, possibly old and ugly, pots of stone. Such a large group needed plenty of water for washing, so there were six containers for this purpose. Indicating these, Jesus said to the servants, "Fill the waterpots with water." The Bible says they filled them *to the brim.* Then Jesus said, "Draw out now and bear them unto the governor of the feast." And they did so.

Somewhere in the process the water had turned to wine. Returning to Matthew Henry's question, "Has your water been turned to wine?" you might answer, "*My* water? I have nothing fit to turn to wine. I muddied my water when I was young. My supply has steadily dwindled. I'm lucky even to have water. Any kind of water. I wouldn't dare ask for wine." Yes, but remember it wasn't the water that was special. It was Christ. He could have made wine out of the water after it was used if he'd wanted to.

You might argue that your vessel isn't fit to make wine in. Perhaps you've marred your body and stained it. Don't you think that old stone waterpot was marred and stained? It wasn't the vessel that held the water nor was it the water in the vessel that produced the miracle. Any old waterpot would have done as well.

He told the servants to fill the waterpots to the brim. "What?" you ask. "Take this dirty water and fill this ugly pot to the brim? Will that work a miracle?" I believe it will. I believe Christ wants us to take what we have and use it to the utmost. If you keep your eyes on the poor quality of your water, it dwindles away. Fill your waterpot, your life, full to the brim, and leave the rest to Christ.

When he has mysteriously turned your water into wine, he will say to you, "Draw out now and bear it. Take it and serve it." You won't discover that your water is turned into wine until you serve it. Draw out generously. Give.

He has more.

Whoever loses his life for my sake will save it, but whoever insists on keeping his life will lose it (Luke 9:24, TLB).

Savior, I confess that I haven't allowed you to turn my life into a life of joyous giving to others. Take my water and turn it into wine. Amen.

Someone Prayed

We had just seen the film, "Corrie," and had moved into the sanctuary for our annual New Year's Eve heritage hymn sing. This would be followed by a devotional message and prayer and climaxed by the organ chimes and the choir's singing of Handel's "Hallelujah Chorus" at the hour of twelve.

The choir filed in to the strains of the organ, but a high-pitched squeal demanded the full attention of every worshiper. Even after the organist stopped playing, the squeal continued.

Our choir director, Jim Davies, bravely began to give the history of "Let All the World in Every Corner Sing," a hymn written by Robert G. McCutchan a hundred years ago. I wanted to listen but couldn't. That squeal distracted me completely. Jim gave Gordie, the organist, the signal to use the piano.

After we had sung that song, Jim reminded us of the story he had told us the week before, how Franz Gruber, the musician, and Joseph Mohr, the pastor, had given the world its best-loved Christmas hymn. *Their* organ wasn't functioning and it became necessary to write something with simple chords that would lend itself to the guitar—the only instrument left for their use. And so "Silent Night" was written for, and first sung to, the guitar. Jim pointed out how fortunate we were to have the grand piano. "The organ seems to have a cipher," he said, explaining that a cipher was a valve that doesn't shut off in a pipe.

Eventually, the squeal stopped. What a relief! But

no, that wasn't the end of the distraction. Jim, no doubt in an effort to test it, had moved over to the organ and had apparently turned it on. The squeal began at once, and didn't cease even though he promptly shut the organ off again. I could only imagine how anxious he was to get it to work properly. The choir had never before been without it for the singing of "The Hallelujah Chorus." And what about the organ chimes on the hour of twelve?

It was now 11:15. Jim introduced another song by giving its history, but I didn't hear a word. The choir and congregation together sang "Day Is Dying in the West." Jim moved back and forth from his place in the loft to the organ, and several times spoke to Gordie as he played the piano, which seemed to bother me more than Gordie. We sang:

> How wonderful it is to come in perfect
> bliss,
> With saints in sweet communion, to such
> a feast as this.   Nils Frykman

I was starting to feel very disappointed with this service. I don't know where the thought came from, but gradually I realized, "Satan's doing this. All this distraction is caused by Satan to keep God from being glorified in our hearts. We came here, some from other congregations, to have a blessed hour together with the Lord as the year turned, but Satan's spoiling it."

My mind went back to Christmas about ten years earlier when our five children all still lived at home. We had pooled our money and bought a small stereo for forty-five dollars at Underwriters' Salvage, where fire-damaged goods were sold to insurance company employees, of which my husband was one.

What joy that stereo had brought us! I'd given Clint, my husband, Handel's *Messiah* on record. Elliot, our son, had recently sung that oratorio with his school singers. He and I loved to sit up late listening to the wonderful choruses and arias. Our favorite solo was "Behold, I show you a mystery. We shall not all sleep, but we shall all be changed, in a moment—in the twinkling of an eye—at the last trumpet."

Then, one evening the machine had refused to play. It was still new, still in its first winter, and here it stood—useless. It wasn't even a pretty piece of furniture.

That evening I had gone to bed quite depressed, and I spoke to God about it: "Lord, I believe you know we have better ways to spend our money than stereo repairs." I thought of the Christian school tuition, the twice-a-year dental bills. "I believe you are pleased that we have our children in the Christian school, and I know you want us to keep all our bills paid. I believe you agree with me that we have better things to do with our money than fix that stereo." Then, as I waited, I thought, "If one of the children were ailing, I'd say, 'Lord, please heal this child.' " So immediately I prayed, "Lord, please heal the stereo."

With that, I went to sleep. The next morning the stereo worked, and it has continued to work.

This whole episode went through my mind in a flash as I sat there, and the same instant I sent up the prayer, "Lord, heal the organ." I prayed it so that God might get the glory from the worship—so that Satan wouldn't have the victory.

It was 11:25. The heritage hymn-sing was over, five minutes ahead of schedule. The squeal persisted.

Pastor Larsen stepped forward to make an announcement. "At 11:30 we will go on KTIS radio." I thought, "No wonder Jim was so nervous."

I could see now that Jim was using his telephone to call the audio room. What might he be suggesting to the sound engineers? A minute later, Lindvall, our sound technician, walked into view from the back, in the gallery along the right side of the church. He went over to the organ pipes along the front, to the right of the platform. Every eye was on him. The only sound now was the high cry of the organ. He moved his hand back and forth as though doing magic. Apparently he got back the feeling or sound he expected. He reached in and took out a tiny pipe.

The hum stopped.

As he walked away with the offending pipe, a smiling congregation gave him enthusiastic applause.

The lady sitting next to me said, "Someone must have prayed."

Christmas Two Weeks Late

 Christmas, 1976, was over. New Year, 1977, had arrived. The tree was down, the candles back in their boxes. Only the poinsettia remained to remind us of the season.

At this time of year I always go carefully through the Christmas cards we received, reading every verse and personal note. Sometimes I think, "I wonder if they chose that verse especially for us?" and sometimes I know they did. As I go through them, I inspect each card and decide whether it has a pretty enough cover to cut off and use next year for a package decoration. I also examine it to see if I can cut off portions for name tags.

"This one's nice. I'll cut this poinsettia around like this, and this bell—can I take this bell?" I peeked inside. "No, if I take the bell, I'll get the signature of Hazel and part of Woody."

Christmas had been exciting and satisfying. All the children were with us except Elliot and his new bride from California. This was our first Christmas with a grandson present. He seemed to consider it his responsibility to assist each of us in opening our gifts. Very soberly he went from one to the other pulling off a bow here and tearing the tissue there. What fun we had!

But I had to admit, the Christmas message had stirred me only a little this year. No, we hadn't missed church. We went faithfully each Sunday morning and evening, all during Advent. We heard good preaching—our pastor is one of the best. The children's program had been as sweet as usual. I had read the Christmas story in private and several times with family and in church. It had been a blessing of mediocre proportions. It was no one's fault. It just wasn't a high point for me spiritually.

Still looking through the cards, I pulled back one I had tossed aside as not worthy of use for name tags or decorations on next year's packages. It was from Pat and Lyle. Pat's a deeply spiritual Christian, a prayer partner who delights in claiming Matthew 18:19 with me and then watching God answer prayer. I looked at the front of the card. It had no gorgeous poinsettia, no holly, no bells or ivy. Its colors were not vibrant or joyous.

The foreground was tan, brown, and gray. It looked, perhaps, like a gate to a city. Through the opening, in the distance, could be seen a night sky and possibly the buildings of Bethlehem. Proceeding through that opening with their backs to me were a man carrying a staff, and a woman on a donkey.

The verse inside this somber card was the Christmas story according to Luke. I read it from beginning to end. And Christmas 1976 came to me two weeks late.

The Christmas story is more than angels singing in the sky. It includes rejection by an innkeeper and the travail of childbirth. Christmas is the first step in Christ's humiliation which culminated in burial in a borrowed tomb. God born of a woman.

On Christmas I had sung "O Little Town of Bethlehem." This day I entered Bethlehem with a man and a young girl on a donkey, and my soul knew it was for me Christ came.

The Making of a Pastor

Garrett Wilterdink turned from the hospital bed with tears in his eyes. He went to the elevator and pressed the button. Sadness clothed him like a garment as he drove himself to his office at the Ivanhoe Reformed Church in suburban Chicago.

Just out of seminary, he had begun his ministry with the eagerness typical of a young pastor in his first post. Ivanhoe was a church that consisted of mostly young families. Garret took pride in delivering well-prepared sermons. He led Bible studies, performed weddings, called on his people, and sought to minister to the community. All of this exhilarated him. It had been almost a year—a good year. Now this.

Ada, the woman he had just left at the hospital, was the young wife of my brother Jack. They had two girls, seven and nine. A delicately beautiful brunette with flawless complexion and large blue eyes, she had been ill for several weeks. A year earlier she had had surgery after which she felt exceptionally well for several months. "Better than I have for years," she had said. Then in November the pain had returned. She stayed at home until after Christmas, then entered the hospital.

Jack, naturally optimistic and boisterous, had grown quieter, sadder. He was losing Ada.

As Garret drove back to the church, he felt again the inadequacy that had almost paralyzed him when Ada had said, "I'm not going to get well. Jack doesn't tell me this, but I know it."

Garret, himself not yet thirty, looked into her large limpid eyes and understood the fear of the unknown she must be feeling as she looked ahead.

Ada continued. "I'm not sure I'm ready to die. I don't—I never. . . Do you know what I mean?"

"I think so."

"Will you help me?"

He nodded. No words came to him. What could he say? "O dear God, don't fail me now. Tell me what to say."

Ada still spoke. "I want to make sure I'll be ready—when. . ." Her words started with urgency but trailed off as again they stood together over that unknown chasm.

How do you minister to a person who's going to die and wants the gospel made clear? The answer crept into Garret's mind. "Do you know John 3:16?"

She nodded.

"Say it with me. 'For God so loved the world, that he gave his only begotten Son, that whosoever believeth in him should not perish, but have everlasting life.'" Garret spoke gently and somewhat hesitatingly. "God has made the gospel very simple for us, easy to understand. This verse means simply that God gave his best, his only Son—himself, really, to show just how much he loves us. That love will last in this life and beyond."

Ada leaned forward listening, her lips parted, her face deathly white.

"He did this so that we might live forever with him in heaven."

A nurse came in. She placed a thermometer in Ada's mouth, then put her finger on Ada's pulse.

Garret waited.

When the nurse removed the thermometer, Ada asked, "How soon can I have another hypo?"

"I'll check your chart. Is your pain getting bad again?"

"Yes. It's getting real bad."

Garret took her hand. "I'll be back tomorrow."

"And talk to me some more about—" She winced. "OK?"

"Sure. Here's the nurse with your hypo. Maybe you can sleep."

Each day for a week, Garret approached that bedside with a deep sense of personal inadequacy. He had never before ministered to a person with a terminal illness. If only she weren't so young! He felt so sorry for her and her husband and little girls. Each time he returned from that bedside he felt emotionally drained.

Ada was an attentive listener. The more he talked about John 3:16, the more she wanted him to. He repeated the same words over and over, but she savored them each time. He found himself consulting commentaries and searching his own soul each morning before going to the hospital. He had never realized how much there was to say about that verse. He expounded on it word by word and phrase by phrase. He applied it to her personally. "Ada, God loves you today just as much as he did when he died for you. He wants you to share his glory. There's glory in heaven such as we can never even imagine. The Bible says in both the Old and New Testaments that 'eye hath not seen, nor ear heard, neither have entered into the heart of man, the things which God hath prepared for them that love him.' We can have only a foretaste here of that glory, but in heaven it will be completely revealed. We will live in the very presence of our heavenly Father."

Ada's undivided attention gratified him, but she never assured him that she knew she was safe for eternity. This puzzled him. Should he press her for a testimony? He wasn't sure.

One day, Garret stepped into the hospital room and found Ada sleeping. The special nurse said that Ada had slipped into a coma a few hours earlier. Garret had been away from his office and they had not been able to reach him. "Has Jack been here?"

"He just left. He was here all morning and he said he'd be right back."

Garret went over to the bed. What if she never became conscious again? Had he failed her? As he looked at her transparent beauty, her brown hair tied back, her mouth slightly open, he observed the lines of suffering. There was no flesh on her bones anymore. He had tried to help her. Again, feelings of failure reached him. Was it too late to help her now?

He moved a chair to her bed. "O God," he prayed silently, "have mercy on Ada. Take her safely home." He wondered if she could hear him if he would speak. "Ada?" No response. Not a flicker of an eyelid or a trembling of a nerve in the hand he held in his. Was it useless? Leaning forward, he whispered, "Ada, God loves you. Jesus died for your sins. God loved you so much he gave his only Son for you. You do believe this, don't you?"

The young man shook his head as tears of helplessness came into his eyes and voice. Desperately, he cried, "Just believe in Jesus, Ada." But Ada made no visible response.

Garret returned that night and ministered to Jack and other family members who waited near that bed. But Ada didn't rally.

Each day, Garret prayed at that bedside and talked gently to Ada. Nurses entered and left. Shifts changed. When she would speak from her bed it would be in delirium. "The bus is here!" she called out as she had so many times to her little girls as they scrambled to get ready for school.

Then one day she called, "Mother!" and opened her eyes.

A nurse bent over her. "Do you want your mother?"

"Yes. My family. My girls and Jack—and the others."

27

When her mother arrived, Ada said, "Mother, I'm safe in the arms of Jesus. I'm going to heaven."

Later, Garret saw her. Her mind now very clear, Ada told him what John 3:16 meant to her. "I know that God loved me so much he died for me. I'm safe in the arms of Jesus. I'm not afraid to die." Shortly after that, she slipped again into the coma from which she never recovered.

Eight weeks had elapsed since Garret had first sat down by her bed to help her understand the gospel of salvation. He left that bedside for the last time a seasoned pastor. He had faithfully given out the Word and God had applied it to Ada's heart, giving her peace and assurance that she was safe for eternity. In the future, he vowed, he'd be faithful in his role as pastor and minister and look to God for the results.

Today, over twenty years later, Dr. Garret Wilterdink is Professor of Preaching at Western Theological Seminary of the Reformed Church in America, Holland, Michigan, where young men are being prepared for the pastoral ministry.

Friendship

She was a nun and he a teenage Protestant.

Their affection for each other began in the 1930s in the high school at Strasburg, North Dakota, later known as the birthplace of Lawrence Welk.

The Catholic community had agreed to make this

school public with the understanding that the nuns would be allowed to stay on as teachers.

None of the rest of us were aware of a special bond between these two—teacher and student. Most of the students liked Sister Consolatrix, and I have never heard of anybody who didn't like John. His zesty voice and hearty laugh resounded in classrooms and halls of the school.

It's hard to estimate how old Sister Consolatrix was. The habit gave her a certain agelessness. She wore rimless glasses. Her straight lips seldom brightened her plain pale face with a smile.

Born and educated in Europe, she had a beautiful soft accent, enchanting to us Hollanders in Strasburg who were accustomed to a heavy German-Russian brogue. I remember her looking up during a study hall to demand, "Who iss murmuring? Who *iss* dat constantly murmuring?" She taught algebra and Latin, and some English. She flitted around wraith-like, swiftly, soundlessly appearing from nowhere. Her favorite word was "Hush!" and in her long white fingers she carried a long white piece of chalk, as though it were an extension of herself.

John was a boisterous Dutchman who had grown to over six feet tall. A sharp dresser, he worked summers to buy his own clothes. He dearly loved life. He had a fondness for women of all ages. And he loved Sister Consolatrix.

The Ursuline Sisters, of whom Consolatrix was one, left Strasburg in 1943. My brother, by then called Jack, had gone to Chicago and had taken up bricklaying. He lost track of Sister, but kept wondering about her. On one of his visits to Strasburg he learned that she had retired to the convent at Belleville, Illinois.

Financial reverses forced Jack to the brink of bankruptcy. In spite of reduced operations, he gradually paid off his creditors. For one of such a sunny nature, he had a hard life. His wife died in 1955, leaving him with two daughters aged seven and nine. He remarried four years later. His second wife brought a son into the family.

The joy of creating with bricks never got old for Jack. Each time I visited Chicago he would drive me around to his project at the time—a store, a house, a church. "It stands there. It will be there long after I'm gone," he'd say.

Trouble couldn't hold Jack down. But there was more on the way. He was being plagued with backaches. In 1969 Jack learned he had a spot on a lung. He had smoked heavily for thirty years. Now no one told him to quit. No surgery was planned; they would keep an eye on it.

Jack and his wife had not been able to travel much. Always intrigued by the history of the South, Jack now proceeded to plan a long vacation. He remembered his favorite teacher.

At Belleville, Jack and Sister Consolatrix had a sweet reunion. They held each other and Jack kissed her.

"How good it is to see you, John," she said. "Sit down and tell me all about yourself and your family. Where is Bessie and how are your parents? And Ruth—where is she?"

She told him she would be traveling through Chicago soon on her way to Germany.

"If you'll let me know when you're going through, I'll come to O'Hare to say good-bye to you," Jack promised.

"I'll write you, John. I surely will."

"What are you going to do in Germany, Sister?"

"Our sisters have a school of 1,000 girls at Aachen. To start with, I'll be giving private lessons in French. Perhaps later, English—German—Latin."

"Great! Wonderful! I'm glad your teaching days aren't over. You're a wonderful teacher, Sister." He had thought she had retired for good.

In the spring the letter came, giving him the time she would arrive at the world's busiest airport.

That afternoon he left work early, speeded to O'Hare, and, finding no place nearby, parked far away. In the terminal he breathlessly asked directions to the gate at which she was to board her plane. That, too, was far, and he knew she'd be boarding soon. Would she wait? He sprinted down the concourse.

He found her there, waiting, even though everyone else had boarded. "I knew you'd come," she said simply. "But now I must board."

Jack took her long delicate hand in both of his huge hands and looked with tenderness into the face of his little teacher for what he felt sure would be the last time. "God keep you, Sister." He kissed her again.

They both promised to write. "After I get settled," Sister said.

The backache which had first brought Jack to the doctor now attacked again with great severity. The spot on his lung had grown larger and was diagnosed as an incurable, inoperable tumor.

Relatives and friends took Jack to the hospital daily for cobalt. After many treatments, which made him very sick, the tumor went down. Then it came back and he had to have cesium. Relief was temporary. There was nothing more that could be done for Jack.

31

His robust voice and hearty laugh were gone, reduced to a whisper and a faint smile. In August of 1971 he died. He'd never again heard from Sister Consolatrix.

By inquiring of my Catholic friends, I learned the address of the convent in Belleville. I wrote the sisters there and received the following information: In Germany Sister Consolatrix had worked as hard as her eighty-two years would allow, teaching private lessons in French and supervising study halls. ("Hush! Who iss dat murmuring?") Suddenly, her strength gave out, and after an illness of two weeks, on July 7, 1969, she had died.

A translation of the obituary written about Sister Consolatrix by a Sister in Germany reveals a reference to Jack: "That she was esteemed by her students is proven by an incident that happened in Chicago. Shortly before her flight to Germany, a middle-aged man ran to Sister Consolatrix to see her once more and to thank her for all she had done for him and for others when he was her student."

These friends of many years, who both had trusted Christ, had their final reunion in heaven, and perhaps were surprised to find each other there so soon. The sweet affection they had for each other had lasted for thirty-five years and could only develop into a deeper kinship in Christ throughout eternity.

Will You Know Your Spouse in Heaven?

Our "Dutch girls" were having a luncheon. Seven of us, friends for a quarter of a century, had come together to compare notes on our lives. Most of us were in our fifties. We had each seen some of our acquaintances widowed.

We got on the subject of how we would manage if our husbands were to die. We agreed that a woman copes better than a man does if left alone. One bright-eyed, pug-nosed gal with a decided middle-age spread said, "George says if I die first he'll move into a little apartment. I told him to find a young, pretty girl and get married again."

"Well," I hedged, "not *too* young or *too* pretty."

We all laughed, our dentures glistening, our eyes twinkling behind their bifocals.

One of the girls asked, "Do you think we'll know each other in heaven? I know the Bible says we won't be *married* in heaven. Do you think husbands and wives will be like everybody else? I mean—"

One of the girls told the story of a little old lady who with cracking voice asked her husband, "Do you think you'll know me in heaven?" Slightly irritated, he retorted, "I should hope so! I know you here, don't I? I don't expect to know less in heaven."

So we talked about heaven. I said I was hoping to get into the same camp with Clint anyway. Since we seemed to grow spiritually at about the same rate, I thought it very possible we'd share a room in heaven. If heaven is perfect for everyone, the pint-sized

Christian will be full and the quart-sized Christian will be full, but as I see it, they might not be in the same camp in heaven. That's merely conjecture, of course.

One of the girls said she didn't think our husbands would be any different to us from anyone else in heaven. Even though she believed this, she felt somewhat cheated. She said she would miss the closeness of the physical side of marriage which we have on earth.

I did a lot of thinking about this on my way home that day. The highest moments of joy and ecstasy on earth I have experienced have been with Clint. But if I'm going to be honest, I have to admit that my lowest moments of misery and sorrow have been with him too. The reverse is also true. No one can make Clint as happy as I can. And no one can make him so miserable.

So how will it be in heaven?

In heaven, both of us will have perfect knowledge of each other, of our past together, and of our future. We will understand everything about each other. Those habits that irritate, those hurts that recur, those doubts that perplex will be swept away like cobwebs. With God-like clarity, I will at last understand the whys. At long last, I will completely understand Clint and be completely understood by him. We will see each other with new vision.

In our marriage we shared our spiritual insights. How many times in reading the Bible together have I looked up and said to Clint, "Imagine that! Isn't that wonderful?" Hundreds of times we have risen from our knees and kissed in deeper understanding—a hint of heavenly fellowship. When deeply stirred by music or sacred songs, in church and at concerts, we have looked into each other's eyes glistening with tears and each understood how the other was moved. Sermons and books that we shared have taken us to a new level of understanding of God. Together we enjoyed Christ and matured in him.

And who would have me believe that in heaven Clint won't be special to me? I concede that I won't be physically married to him there, but I won't be cheated, for I'll have a new heavenly body. Without our biological drives and appetites, we won't miss sex any more than we'll miss peanut butter. In heaven we won't have the hurts, the fears, the anxieties and misunderstandings that make the act of love on earth so necessary and rewarding. In heaven I expect to enjoy Clint completely without any setbacks caused by human frailty.

If he gets there first, I sort of expect he'll be at the gate with that warm, tender smile on his face. He'll have so much to show me—so many people he'll want me to meet. He'll be excited. He always likes to show me something he has discovered first, and then explain it to me. When our emotions get too much for us, we'll look at each other, perhaps through tears, and I'll hear him say, "Isn't it wonderful, Mother?" And I'll squeeze his hand.

And when our children start joining us up there, it will be special to Clint and me. And it will be special for them. Imagine our son David arriving there, expecting to see both of us, and finding me alone, asking, "Where's Dad?"

"Well, Son, he'd like to have been here, but you see he was called away on another assignment." No, I don't think God would deny us the privilege of both being there when our children come home.

Suppose one of our five had been a little slow

about making up his mind about following Jesus. Suppose we had both died before that one had definitely made his commitment. Perhaps it would be years later that heaven would ring with rejoicing because the last one had finally cast herself totally on the Lord Jesus Christ. Then, when she made it home, Clint and I would be waiting for her together.

It wouldn't be the first time, I assure you. Whenever any of our children are on their way home, whether from college or from their work, both Clint and I lay aside every project as we wait for them. When "They're here!" rings out, we scramble for the door from wherever we are.

You say we'll all love each other the same in heaven—that I'll love you, and Clint will love you as much as Clint and I will love each other? Then it's not that Clint and I will love each other *less* in heaven, but that we will love you *more*.

In that case, we'll all be the richer for it, won't we? I can just hear Clint say, "Isn't it wonderful, Mother?"

Nailbiting

A few months earlier, my Nella had been a bubbling two-year-old. But that was before Brian came along.

Brian had upset her feelings of security. Not only did he take an awful lot of Mommy's time, but Daddy also made a big fuss over him. Grace and Elliot seemed to like Brian better because they fought over who might hold him. But the thing that bothered Nella most was the time when this little usurper had exclusive rights to Mommy. Four times a day he nursed at her breast!

That little stranger surely made Mommy busy and impatient and cross. Nella began to withdraw. She became shy and serious and began to bite her nails.

Oh how guilty Nella's problem made me feel! It was pretty obvious that I wasn't providing for all her emotional needs, but I couldn't blame myself too much. I wasn't wasting my twenty-four hours a day. I never got all the rest I needed even though I tried to catch up when the children napped.

Determined to do something about that nailbiting, I began to find time to play more with Nella. I talked with her and read to her. But she still chewed her nails.

I tried to make her proud of pretty fingernails by keeping polish on them. I gave her chewing gum in the hope she'd become so occupied she wouldn't bite her nails. Weeks went by. Nella seemed determined to keep her bad habit.

I admitted defeat. "What shall I do?" I cried out. *"If any lack wisdom, let him ask of Me."*

I waited for a suggestion. Prayerfully I did my duties for my family. Afternoon came and I proceeded to put Nella and Brian down for naps, hardly able to wait until I could lie down for a while myself. Then the message from heaven came through. "Why don't you take Nella to bed with you instead of putting her in her own bed?"

Of course! Why hadn't I thought of that?

That day Nella and I nursed brother together and then transferred him to his own bed to sleep. Nella stayed with me. I held her close to me, cradling in my arms her little head with its fine brown hair.

We did this the rest of that winter. During the

minutes before sleep, I would playfully say: "Nella, next time you want to bite your nails, say to yourself, 'Don't be silly! I don't have to bite my nails! My mommy loves me!'" Then we would both giggle and go to sleep to the rhythm of our breathing.

From time to time after that I would see her start to bite a nail, then remember, and look at me. Slanting her eyes at me most becomingly she would say, "Don't be silly. My mommy loves me." Then she would giggle and go on playing.

In a few weeks, not only were Nella's nails grown out, but she was much happier. That hour in my arms gave her the comfort and security she needed. And it did a lot for me, too.

Happy Birthday, Dear Neighbor

My elderly neighbor wasn't exactly sure of her age, but she knew she was soon to have a birthday. "They always take my picture with my cake," she said over and over.

But her sons and daughters were feuding among themselves. I wasn't the least bit sure there would be a party this year. I didn't want to prepare for one if the children were planning anything, but the closer we came to the much-anticipated event, the less likely it seemed that any party was being planned.

So I ordered a cake. I figured if none of her own family would come to celebrate with her, I'd bring my own five eager children over. They would be glad to share cake and party with her.

The day of her birthday arrived. I had barely entered her house when I heard her call from her room to her bachelor son, "George! George! Mrs. Peterman is here. Show her my cake!"

I arrived at her room at the same moment George entered with the cake. It was really beautiful, topped with gooey pink rosebuds and "Happy Birthday, Neighbor" in green icing.

"What more could I want?" she exclaimed. "It's just too beautiful." Turning to me with dancing eyes she said, "Did you know that Karen and Hilda are coming?" Karen was her niece, and Cousin Hilda was about her own age.

"Good! We'll have a party. What time?"

"Two o'clock! They said they'd be here at two o'clock. And Hilda always brings presents. I know she'll have a nice present for me. Hilda gives *nice* things!"

I started to get excited. I checked the freezer. Plenty of ice cream. Whom else could I invite? The next-door neighbors agreed to come. At noon, one of her sons who lived in an adjacent suburb called and said he and his wife and their two children would see her a little later. It looked like it might yet be a real party.

She started getting ready before noon. She proceeded to examine all of her stockings. She had just come through a long period of illness which had kept her at home for many months. She hadn't needed new clothes. Now at last she found a pair of hose without runs.

She carefully laid out her undergarments and then went to the closet. After much indecision, she chose a slightly soiled white brocade dress. Then I helped her dress.

The corset almost slipped down over her hips, as

she had lost much weight. She needed it only to hold up her stockings. I pulled the hose over her feet and attached the hose to their garters. Then came her undergarments, and finally the dress. By one o'clock, she had been metamorphosed into an elegant dowager bedecked with long-tucked-away diamonds and pearls. I combed her hair, which I had pinned up for her the night before.

"You're as pretty as a picture," I said.

"Oh, they'll take my picture," she said, as though I might have hinted they would not. "They *always* take my picture."

I just hoped they wouldn't forget.

From one until two o'clock, she sat at her dresser and tried various pieces of jewelry on and off again. The pearls finally gave place to a cheap pair of pink rope beads which she looped over her head to form a double strand. She found rhinestone earrings which she managed to get on her ears. Then she lifted the tray of jewelry and from underneath took two rhinestone sidecombs which she stuck into her hair on both sides. She turned sideways for my inspection.

"Just right," I said.

She lowered her eyes and smiled. Looking at her watch, she shook it. "Is it only 1:30? Time sure goes slow!"

She took out the combs, rearranged her hair, and in so doing messed it all up. She put the combs back in and then searched through a box of miscellaneous articles until she found a sample tube of lipstick. She applied it to her top lip, then rubbed her lips together. It was orange. She turned to me once more. I smiled.

Promptly at two the elderly cousin arrived with her daughter. The two cousins hugged each other as the expected present transferred hands.

Then the doorbell announced the arrival of the neighbors. At 2:30 her son Clyde, whom I had never seen before, arrived with his family.

I noted that George stayed in his room, and I gathered that he and Clyde were not on speaking terms.

I had set the table with the cake in the center and my neighbor's gifts at her place. We sang "Happy Birthday to You" and my neighbor looked happily embarrassed.

The picture! I hadn't seen anyone bring in a camera. I looked carefully around. There was no camera anywhere.

"Uh—why don't you open your gifts while I get the coffee?" I suggested. I brought her a pair of scissors and then quietly slipped out the door to my own house across the street.

Moments later, when I returned, I snapped a picture of her taking her last gift out of the box. It was a luxurious, pale pink cotton sweater from her cousin. When all the wrappings were cleared away I took a picture of her with her cake and another one of everyone seated at the table. Then the happy birthday lady demanded, "Now let's have some of that beautiful cake!"

She didn't converse, but ate silently. She seemed very happy. Her eyes were bright and her cheeks flushed with excitement. I had never seen her so lovely.

If my friend missed anyone that day, there was no sign of it. Her aged face showed only satisfaction and contentment. She had had her cake and her party and we had taken her picture.

Two weeks later she died.

Home on His Shoulder

The telephone jangled raucously. I put on the light and checked the clock. Three in the morning. "Hello."

"This is George. Could you come over a minute? Mother's partly on and partly off the bed. She's sleeping so soundly I can't wake her."

This sounded familiar. When I was a teenager I had slept in the same bedroom with my grandmother and had seen her sustain several strokes.

Clint and I went across the street. I heard the snoring-blowing sound before I got upstairs to her room. We lifted her back onto her bed. She still had the curlers in her hair which I had put there the evening before. We had agreed I would give her a permanent next week. When I had washed her hair, I had accidentally got her quite wet. So after we had finished, she quipped, "I almost went under for the third time."

Now we tried to waken her, but she made no sign of even hearing us. George called the doctor. He would send an ambulance. We waited. I washed her face with a cool cloth and took the curlers out of her hair.

Strange, I thought, that I should be the one to stand at her bed doing this when she has four daughters, two of them living right in the city. But then, perhaps not so strange.

A few weeks ago, my elderly neighbor had said, "I get so lonesome for my girls." She asked me to find a pen and some paper. Then she dictated a letter to one of her daughters who lived in a small town in Minnesota. She explained that she couldn't write because she shook too much. Then she talked at length about her wonderful "nurse" who was so kind to her. I shortened this part considerably. She didn't complain or beg for attention. She just shared how she was feeling and said good-bye. Even though I took care of her every day after that, I never saw an answer to her letter.

One of the two daughters in our city had come over a few times in the months I took care of her mother. She had come the day *after* her mother's birthday party. Her mother had carefully saved a piece of the cake for her.

I had never seen the other girl. There appeared to be some secret my neighbor kept from me about this daughter. She would refer to Stella from time to time, but she always seemed to stop talking about Stella just before she might divulge something private. She would look away and stare into space. I wondered. Had Stella shamed the family or hurt them badly? I never learned what it was. Even in senility, my neighbor guarded her secret.

Now I remembered that I had been the last person to wash and set her hair. It was I who had shared her last meal. I had given her her last kiss.

George and Clint were talking. "I don't think the minister can get here before the ambulance comes," George said.

The minister. Did George want someone to pray for his mother?

"George, would you like me to pray?"

"Oh yes, would you?"

I nodded. We drew our chairs up to the bed. I picked up her Bible and opened it to Psalm 23, her favorite. "Dear Shepherd," I prayed, "please take this your child safely through the valley of the shadow of death and home to your fold."

The ambulance stopped out front. George declined our offer to meet him at the hospital. We went home.

As we went, I prayed that there would be someone to stand with my parents to commend them to God—should I not arrive in time.

And when he hath found [the sheep], he layeth it on his shoulders, rejoicing (Luke 15:5).

Lord, I pray for every dying saint, knowing that you will carry each one safely through the valley of the shadow of death. Amen.

My father died July 19, 1973, after a long illness. Dorothy Rodenburg, my husband's sister, stayed with him, as none of his children were able to be there.

Prayer Meeting

*Lord, I think you know
Why I didn't join
my fellow believers in their pleas,
"Come quickly, Lord Jesus."*

*I believe you know
It's not that I'm unprepared.
I've paid my vows.*

My conscience doesn't rebuke me.
I've testified to the world
And before the congregation
Of your saving love,
Bearing witness to what you've done
For me.

And, Lord, I do appreciate it.
How often
You've reinstated me
When my feet slipped.

Today, there's no blemish
or scar
Left from my sins.
You washed me clean
And dressed me in white.

Neither is it that there's one
I might tell of your grace
Whom I haven't yet told—

I know of no harsh word
To call back;
No forgiveness
To seek
or to give.

My work? It will all be done
Whenever you come for me.
Lord,
You be the judge of that.

Why then can't I join this joyous chant,
"Come quickly"?
You know, don't you, Lord?

If you should come today,
Not all my loved ones
Would go with us.

Crying

Elliot and Joey had gone for a bike ride. When they were far from home, Elliot swerved too suddenly and toppled to the ground, sliding across the pavement, burning elbows, knees, and forehead.

He made a depressing picture as he entered the house—jeans torn, perspiration and blood on his forehead, water oozing from a blackened elbow and knee.

We crowded around him, comforting and soothing him. I cleaned each bruise and applied salve and bandages.

When there was a lull in the excitement, six-year-old Brian throatily asked, "Did Joey cry for you, Elliot?"

"No," Elliot replied simply.

"I would've."

I wonder if this world isn't weighed down under so much suffering because Christians aren't crying. Our society is torn by racial strife, mental and physical illness, moral degeneracy, and war. Hearts ache and break.

Can I weep for the man who suffers at the hands of another, whether he is white or black? Can I sympathize with the teenager whose confusion causes him to experiment with drugs?

Do I see the lostness of my generation? When Christ met stubborn resistance to his spiritual ministry, he wept. The Apostle Paul had great heaviness and continual sorrow in his heart when he thought of his kinsmen who refused to acknowledge Christ as their Messiah. Do I have this sorrow for neighbors and friends who aren't Christians?

Did not I weep for him that was in trouble? Was not my soul grieved for the poor? (Job 30:25).

Father, keep our hearts tender that we may remember not only to rejoice with those who rejoice but also to weep with those who weep. Amen.

Emergency

When our children were little, we lived on a busy one-way street. As soon as our toddlers were permitted freedom, we mothers attempted to instill in them great respect for the avalanche of cars that rushed by our homes, especially between four and six in the afternoon.

I remember those little warnings that used to flash into my mind: "Better check on Gracie" (or Elliot, or Nella—which ever one was little at the time). I made it a rule to follow that hunch as soon as possible. Often I'd find them playing too near the curb.

As they grew older and started school, I often got those little reminders to check on their safety. But they were out of my hands and in the care of teachers and the safety patrol. Soon I learned to pray whenever I had the feeling that they were in trouble. I began to think, "When I can't go myself, I'll send God."

As the older children spent more and more of their time away from home, I spent more and more time in prayer. I didn't sit down to pray very often, but I learned what it was to pray almost without ceasing. While I had the children at home, I taught them all I could. I was no longer able to answer all their calls for help when they were in real danger; I wasn't able to warn them of every possible hazard that existed. I had to develop a strong trust in God.

One evening a neighbor boy knocked loudly at our door as he hollered, "David's hurt! He's stuck in his wagon down at the old church." As I ran along with him, I could hear David screaming.

By letting down the handle of the wagon I was able to release David's finger. When he saw he wasn't bleeding, he stopped crying and rubbed away his tears. As soon as he could he said, "Mommy, I'm so glad you're here. I couldn't come myself, so I sent my friend."

As I pulled David home in that wagon I realized that life for him was just beginning. Where would it take him? I thought of the usual physical and moral threats to a boy. I shuddered as I thought of Vietnam. Would I be able to trust God to answer the calls of David, my youngest, even from a battlefield?

Lifting his brown eyes, he said, "You always come when I call for you, don't you?"

I pulled the wagon back into our yard. Thoughtfully I answered him, "If there's ever a time that I can't come myself, David, I'll send my Friend."

As one whom his mother comforteth, so will I comfort you (Isaiah 66:13).

Father, you are the God of ourselves and our children. Give us the faith to believe you will be to them everything we have been—and more. Amen.

Going Down Devil's Hill

"Stop!" I cried, but I knew he couldn't. His expression of glee changed to terror as the pedals of his tricycle flew around so fast that his feet no longer could find them.

Faster and faster the trike rolled down the hill. I cut a diagonal line toward him, but he was too far away for me to reach him. "Lord God, Lord God, Lord God," I prayed. David's little form in his blue chambray shirt, still upright on the red trike, vanished over the steepest part of the hill.

I was familiar with this park. At the base of the hill (called Devil's Hill) ran a sidewalk, on the outside of which was a cement curb. This curb, I knew, would stop my five-year-old son's trike. His life or death would depend on how he hit that curb.

Then I saw him again. Still upright, the trike

dropped from the grass onto the bare ground where grass had been trimmed from around the walk, then leaped up onto the sidewalk, and smashed into the curb. The impact hurled David and his trike into the air and forward, tossing him lightly onto the soft green earth.

As if God couldn't wait to give me my answer, David bounced up onto his feet. His lusty screaming assured me he wasn't seriously injured.

When I finally reached him, I didn't seize him or clutch him to me. I just looked closely at him. There was not a bruise or smudge on him anywhere.

As David's screams subsided, I asked, "What made you turn off the sidewalk and go down the hill?"

"I just thought of it," he whimpered.

The thought had been the act. A sharp turn to the left in a careless moment had sent him speeding downward to what could have been destruction. Yet God had spared him.

How dear he seemed to me. I touched his face and kissed his hair, and pressed his pounding heart against mine. At last, in the stillness of the park occupied only by ourselves, we knelt and thanked our heavenly Father for sparing David's life.

As we walked the six blocks from the park to our home, pulling the injured trike, I saw something symbolic in this miraculous physical salvation of my son. Should David ever in life be proceeding safely and happily along a certain course, and then make a sharp turn downward—should he then wish to stop, and find his will impotent to do so—surely God could again bring him to a stop without a mark upon him.

Once more I prayed for my son, "Lord God." Again, I knew he had heard.

This poor man cried, and the Lord heard him, and saved him out of all his troubles (Psalm 34:6).

Father, we thank you that all we have to do is call upon your name and you hear us. Amen.

Intercession

The day I heard that a daughter of my aged friends had died and was already buried, I rushed to their home.

Mrs. Nardine stood at the door, tall, thin, and bent, her eyes red from weeping, her gray-yellow hair disheveled.

We held each other. "I didn't know," I apologized. "I first found out about it at—"

"I understand," she answered.

I could see her husband at the table in the kitchen. "Were you having breakfast?"

"No, we have finished. We were just having our morning devotions. But we can wait. Sit down."

"I'll join you in the kitchen and pray with you," I said.

I kissed her husband and accepted a chair at the table. "What did she die of?" I asked.

The mother looked squarely into my eyes and gave what seemed her prepared answer. "This is the daughter that had cancer twice." Her eyes held mine. She hesitated as though waiting for that to sink in. "She died because she couldn't face life anymore."

I had heard, but hadn't grasped what she was say-

51

ing. If I hadn't noticed the resoluteness of her speech, I would have questioned her further. Then the truth occurred to me.

"I understand," I said.

"That's what makes it so much harder. It would be hard anyway, but this—" She was using her handkerchief freely now. The old man stared blankly at her.

The daughter had told her sister after the second cancer operation that she'd never put her family through the expense and anguish again. They now believed she had found signs of a recurrence of the disease.

We talked for twenty minutes. Then I said, "I'll have to leave quite soon. Would you like me to stay for your devotions?"

Apparently the doorbell had interrupted Mrs. Nardine in the middle of a sentence, for now she continued her prayer. "And, Lord, we ask you to be with the Ogdahls in Congo. Bless their children away at school and may the money be raised for a church building. Bless the Jordahls in Ecuador and the Smiths in Peru as they translate the Scriptures so the natives may learn your Word. Be with Spike behind the Iron Curtain. . ."

I peeked to see if she were reading or following notes. No, all of this was from memory. She prayed around the world, naming missionaries and places I'd never heard of. It was clear this was a well-established custom.

The Nardines had two sons who were foreign missionaries. I wondered if the parents' interest in missions stemmed from that, or whether the boys had become missionaries as a result of a home that prayed thus for missionaries.

Mrs. Nardine had finished praying for missions

and now proceeded to pray for her own family. Her voice changed key; it faltered a bit from time to time. She lifted her glasses and wiped her eyes. When she finished, I had the feeling that now even God knew their plight better than before.

Then I prayed with them. Afterward they both clung to me, the old lady tearfully speaking of God's faithfulness in trouble. The old man thanked me for coming.

I'll long remember the faith I witnessed that day, faith that prayed for missionaries when the hearts of the intercessors were breaking with their own sorrow.

Perhaps Today

I was waiting for a bus. Snow swirled around my feet. Wind stung my face. Judging from the number of people waiting, it seemed the bus was already late. People pulled themselves inside collars and hoods. One man sought shelter under a canopy and tried to read the paper. Every so often someone would leave the group and saunter to the curb, where he would strain his eyes to see if a bus was in sight. The man who was reading the paper looked up from time to time and glanced up the street, always in the same direction. Those who had withdrawn into their collars and hoods might have been hibernating were it not for the air of expectancy about them. Everyone seemed to know the bus was coming. Even when it was blocks away, the group slowly started changing formation. Wordlessly, every person in the group slowly drew to the curb and stood in readiness for the door to open and receive him out of the storm.

This little scene is reenacted in various ways by millions of people who wait every day for buses and trains. They wait expectantly. They may seem to be occupied with something else; they may appear to be asleep; but let that bus arrive, and no one misses it. All are singlemindedly waiting for it.

Each time I wait for a bus I realize that this should be our attitude toward Christ's return. Christ said, "Watch therefore: for ye know not what hour your Lord doth come. Therefore be ye also ready: for in such an hour as ye think not the Son of man cometh."

I have to admit that sometimes I don't think of Christ's return for a whole day. Sometimes I give it a passing thought only once or twice a week. Doing my daily work, coping with my daily problems, I become so involved that the "blessed hope" of Christ's return doesn't govern my life.

One day as I sat in the living room of a stranger waiting for her to get out her checkbook and make a donation to a community drive I represented, I noticed a tiny plaque propped up on her end table. It said, "PERHAPS TODAY." That's all.

Perhaps today Christ will return. If I really believed that, my attitude would be eager and expectant. There would be things I'd want to get done *first*, like witnessing to that loved one still without Christ.

Since I wouldn't be *sure* he'd come today, I would still have to do my work and live as though I might enjoy old age; but my attitude in doing so would be different. Perhaps today. Perhaps not. More of my earnings should go into missions. I should take more time to tell others about Christ's redeeming love. More of my writing should be directed toward eternal goals. I should be more careful in speech and conduct. Earthly pleasures would hold less charm.

Paul wrote to Titus that "denying ungodliness and worldly lusts, we should live soberly, righteously, and godly, in this present world; looking for that blessed hope, and the glorious appearing of the great God and our Saviour Jesus Christ; Who gave himself for us, that he might redeem us from all iniquity, and purify unto himself a . . . people, zealous of good works" (Titus 2:12-14).

I want to develop an attitude of "looking for that blessed hope." One day the great God and our Savior Jesus Christ will appear and take me out of the storm. Not only that, but there is "a crown of righteousness, which the Lord . . . shall give me at that day: and not to me only, but unto all them also that love his appearing" (2 Timothy 4:8). Do you?

Lord, I realize afresh that you could return today. Help me to focus on that hope. Amen.

Interruption

After I'd sent my publisher my manuscript for the book, *Held for Ransom,* on the Kronholm kidnapping, my editor called. "We'd like you to go beyond Eunice's release and tell of the second kidnap attempt on both her and Gunnar, and go into the trials and all that."

I managed to secure copies of the court transcripts and proceeded to settle in for another six weeks or more of work. Eunice and Gunnar prepared tapes for me, and upon receiving these I knew at once which episode I'd write first. With Gunnar's specific account of the second kidnap attempt, I couldn't wait to get to my typewriter.

In this scene, Gunnar and Eunice had just returned from their annual trip to Washington, D. C. It's late, and before going to bed, Gunnar checks the house. He goes into the furnace room, a four-by-five room containing the furnace and a trap door to a crawl space under the house. He's becoming increasingly uneasy. Something's telling him to keep checking. As he surveys the trap door, he notices that the two hasps by which the trap door is lifted are in improper position. Now, very suspicious, and seized with cold fear, Gunnar goes into that crawl space. The light is out! It should have come on with the one in the furnace room. The need to know pushes him forward. I write, "He walked stealthily to where the crawl space formed an 'L' and threw the beam of the flashlight over there. All he saw was camping equipment and Christmas decorations. As he started back from the step to go up from the crawl space, he threw the light to the front of the area. Here was the six-foot base of the fireplace of the family room.

"Two feet disappeared suddenly behind the fireplace base.

" 'Dear God,' " he prayed, 'we have company!' Gunnar's hair jerked in its roots. Cold, clammy sweat gathered in pools all over his body."

I wrote about his calling Eunice to bring the gun. As Gunnar called the police, he kept an eye on the trap door to the crawl space. Then, "The trap door was starting to move. Gunnar dropped the phone and Eunice handed him the gun. Jamming a shell into it, Brian shouted—"

There I stopped and looked at what I'd written: BRIAN? I stared at the name in the space where Gunnar's should have appeared. I was thinking Gunnar and had written Brian. Why, there was no Brian in this scene, nor in any I'd written the last few days. Whatever made me write *Brian?*

I stared at it for only a moment. I rose quickly to my feet and began to pray. Our son, Brian, was a junior in college in Wheaton, Illinois. Clint, Dave, Elliot, and I had heard the radio broadcast of Eunice Kronholm's kidnapping as we traveled by car to Indianapolis for Brian's and Terri's wedding. In fact, about the time the kidnappers had forced Eunice into the trunk of a Mark IV Continental, where she'd stayed for eight hours, Brian and Terri were saying their vows in a small church in Indianapolis.

I paced the floor. "Lord, only you know why you wanted me to stop working and pray for Brian. Whatever it is, Lord, you take care of it. If he's driving and there's a drunken driver bearing down on him—if he's unhappy or discouraged, if he's writing a test, if Satan is tempting him in any way, I know you are on Brian's side and I trust you to win the battle."

It would be a dramatic ending if I could say I learned later that Brian remembered that afternoon very well. But that wasn't the case. He couldn't recall any narrow escape from accident or death. He didn't recall being "down" that day, and if anyone had been trying to tempt him to sin, Brian was unaware of it. He could in no way account for my urgency to pray.

I don't believe God was playing a trick on me. I believe Brian was in very imminent danger to his body or soul, even though he remained unaware of it.

How grateful I am to God for keeping me this close to my children. Brian and Terri have since moved to Minneapolis and live a mile from us. Grace and her husband Larry Christensen and Andrew live in Edina, a suburb of Minneapolis; Dave's still at home, working full time. Nella and Rick Hauser live in Wheaton, Illinois; Elliot and Cheryl live in California. How amazing that God alerts me to their needs.

Do parents ever cease to be needed by their children and grandchildren? I think not.

The secret things belong unto the Lord our God: but those things which are revealed belong unto us and to our children for ever, that we may do all the words of this law (Deuteronomy 29:29, KJV).

Lord, I pray that I may live long and that, no matter how wracked up my body may be, I may have a clear enough head to pray for my children and grandchildren, and for any other needs you bring to my attention. Amen.

Signals

Driving through Chicago we paused at a busy intersection that appeared to have about six traffic lights of red and green, plus arrows. In the midst of this confusion, we saw a sign that warned, "Obey Your Own Signals."

That busy intersection spelled confusion until we concentrated on our own signals. Then, with caution, we proceeded safely.

We talked about what excellent advice that was and agreed that heeding it would also make life simpler. The more I thought about it, the more I realized that it's not for lack of signals that this is an age of confusion; but rather, people are seeing too many signals to concentrate on obeying their own.

We have the perfect standard for life and conduct, the Bible. If we become thoroughly acquainted with this book, it will implant within each of us a system of stop-and-go signals. Have you ever felt instinctively that something was right (or wrong) for you and haven't been certain why? Every man's conscience is something of a guide, but a Christian's conscience, if cultivated under the Word of God, becomes a sanctified conscience. His warnings to "stop" and "go" become a valuable and quite reliable guide.

At that intersection there wasn't much time to hesitate. So it is with some decisions in life. We don't always have time to find a chapter and verse to show us clearly whether to go or stop. But we do have a signal within us which, if we obey it, will take us safely across another intersection.

I pondered some of the perplexities of confusing signals. I thought about how hard it was to raise a family in an era when so many parents were excessively permissive. Some neighbor children never had tasks assigned to them. They appeared at our door to play before our children had breakfast. My signal stated, "Small tasks are good for small children," and so I sent the neighbor children home until my own had finished their work.

I also found that Christian parents weren't all

agreed on the spiritual upbringing of their children. Some families had no family prayer or Bible study. Some allowed high school children to neglect Sunday school and worship services. Some grudgingly permitted their children to take Sunday employment. Some children had endless liberty to watch television. Some mothers went to work and relegated their home responsibilities to baby-sitters. Parents everywhere were attending family seminars and PTA meetings searching for more knowledge on how to raise their families. Each set of parents hoped to steer their children through the teens without rebellion. In all of this I witnessed confusion.

Life is full of alternatives. Well-meaning friends and relatives suggest routes we might follow. This applies to where we work and live, how we spend our money, how we train our children. But in the end each person, each parent, must make his own decision.

Nothing settles confusion as much as obeying one's own signals.

And thine ears shall hear a word behind thee, saying, This is the way, walk ye in it (Isaiah 30:21).

Father, help me to watch and listen for your signals. Then give me the courage to proceed without fear. Amen.

Too Late

Ever since entering Minnehaha Academy as a freshman, Nella had set her sights on becoming a cheerleader.

Tryouts had proved that practice pays. For a year she'd gone through the cheers daily, sometimes in the dining room with table and chairs moved to the wall, sometimes on the lawn in spite of the heavy one-way traffic by our house.

Now she was officially a cheerleader! Together we'd sat up late at night sewing her red and white corduroy culottes and vest for her season of cheerleading.

Our entire family went the night of the first game. Clint had brought the camera and had it ready for a shot the instant they started a cheer.

How happy they looked, these six honored ones. Nella, flushed with excitement, was even prettier than usual, her brown hair in a gleaming flip, her black eyes sparkling like gems, her white teeth even and pleasing.

For a moment I looked away from her as I briefly conversed with another proud parent. The band began. I looked back to the cheerleaders and saw them clapping and chanting.

But Nella was no longer with them! I looked hard at the uniformed girls. I counted them—there were only five. They looked happy and confident. I could hardly stand it. Oh, where was she? She'd been there just a moment ago. Unless she came right away, she'd miss the big moment. Tears filled my eyes from my own disappointment.

Then she came. She got in step with her friends and joined in the cheer.

I don't know what personal emergency prevented her from being on the floor when the time came to start cheering. She'd practiced a year for this and had missed the opening.

It was a warning to me. While waiting for Nella to come into her honor, I had thought what it would be like to sit down to the marriage feast of the Lamb and find one of my children missing.

As I watched Nella do the handsprings and flips, I vowed that, with God's help, no negligence of mine would prevent her or any of my five children from answering the roll at that great feast of God.

No latecomers there.

My people are destroyed for lack of knowledge: because thou hast rejected knowledge, I will also reject thee, that thou shalt be no priest to me: seeing thou hast forgotten the law of thy God, I will also forget thy children (Hosea 4:6).

Father, help us parents to instruct our children in the Word and guide them by example. Then give us the confidence that you will move by your Spirit to bring them to repentance for their sins and enable them to live a godly life. May we together share in your joys forever. Amen.

The Old Oaken Rocker

There it lay in the yard, runners up, arms out, as though embracing the pile of junk on which it had been cast. There were no more babies to rock—and it was broken anyway. Even its straw interior hung out. Turning my eyes from its shame, I started breakfast.

As the bacon began to curl on the griddle, I looked once more out of the window at the immense pile of refuse which the men of the family had made the evening before while cleaning the basement. I saw things we had kept for years. On top of it all, in a state of utter dejection and futility, lay the rocker, mute testimony to an era that had slipped away as quietly as my jet black hair had turned partly gray.

I relived years in just a few moments as I looked at the rocker. Emotion crowded out every practical thought. I was back in that chair, feeding my nine-month-old son Elliot. He had been teething and had also been exposed to measles. When his fever went up to 103, I called the doctor.

"Watch for more symptoms," he said. "Meanwhile, give him aspirin every four hours."

Every time Elliot woke from his sleep he wanted only to nurse. When I held him up to my face, he latched onto my chin, rubbing his gums savagely over it. He was very restless, his little face troubled. After days of aspirin, nursing, rocking, and napping, Elliot seemed a little better. One night after dinner, my husband went back to work. For the first time all week, Elliot sat at his toy box and played. Much relieved, I watched him. Gradually I began to feel my own weariness.

Suddenly I became aware that Elliot was playing only with his left hand. Knowing he generally favored the right, I handed him a toy. He reached out with the left hand. I put the toy next to his right hand. He reached over with the left and took the toy. I picked up his right hand and looked at it carefully. When I let it go, it dropped like a rag. With alarm, I telephoned my husband.

I picked up my little son and held him close to me in the rocker. He lay still. His spirit seemed quiet now. His hot little face was lifted up to mine; his bright fevered eyes searched my anxious ones; he did not fall asleep, or even move. We continued thus in the rocker for the half hour that it took for my husband to come home.

Instantly sharing my alarm, he called the doctor. He said that, while it appeared to be polio, he would have to take a spinal tap to be sure. We met him at the hospital.

The spinal count confirmed our fears. The doctor told us that the polio wards in the hospitals had filled up that day, so we would have to take Elliot home for the night.

My son—to hold, and to rock, and to nurse *for one more night!* Then we will take him away. And only our heavenly Father knows how long he'll be gone and what shape he will be in when he returns. Never had I known such sorrow!

We took him to the Sister Elizabeth Kenny Institute the next morning. Sitting in a crowded waiting room, thinking but not speaking, both of us tried to hold part of Elliot.

A white uniform appeared in front of us. "Come with me," the nurse said to my husband, who had the bigger part of Elliot.

I rose to follow.

"You stay here," she said to me.

Raising my eyes to look at the voice, I beheld a severe face. She couldn't know how I felt. A sob caught in my throat.

A few minutes later my husband returned. A clerk informed us we were free to go.

"Won't we see him in his bed—or meet his nurse?" I asked.

"Oh no," she answered. "You won't see him for two weeks. He's in isolation."

We walked stiffly out of the hospital. Outside, our eyes met. My husband's smile had tears in it.

Returning home to the empty house and empty crib, I sank into the rocker with empty arms.

"O God," I prayed, "be father and mother to my unweaned child. Keep him from missing me too much. Ease my grief. All thy waves and thy billows are gone over me."

For the two weeks that he remained in isolation, the image of his little hot and troubled face never left me. Often I sat in the rocker and just cried.

The emotion I had felt fourteen years before gripped me this morning as I stood at my window. I hardly heard the family coming down the stairs.

How could I let that old rocker go?

My husband, delivering his morning kiss, looked into my face with infinite understanding: "Shall I bring it back into the house?"

I shook my head.

"We could probably have it fixed," he persisted.

"No," I said weakly. "It has no value."

"Except that you like it."

I nodded, tears blurring the view of the rocker.

"Come on, Mom, let's eat," begged Elliot from his

place at the table. At fifteen, he was as tall as his father, and almost as strong.

We sat down to our bacon and eggs, garnished with gloom. My self-control gave way as I wailed, "I'll have to go to the neighbors' to rock my grand-children!"

"God forbid," my husband said, reaching across the table to pat my hand. "How would it be if I got you a brand new rocker?"

I stared at my plate. I could chew but not swallow.

"I want my own chair," I whispered. "I don't want a *new* chair. I want my *old* rocker." A salty tear seasoned the egg on my plate.

"You shall have your own chair, Mother," my husband soothed. "We'll have it fixed."

Wiping his mouth with his napkin, he kissed me tenderly. Then, with masterful step, he strode out the door, and retrieved the old oaken rocker from the heap of rubbish.

The Boy with the Arm

"You must be careful not to overshelter him," the doctor warned. This dear family friend continued: "Let him make his own way in the world right away. Don't *ever* consider him 'the boy with the arm.'"

My husband and I nodded. At nine months, Elliot had had polio. For three months we had seen him only on Sundays. We were allowed to embrace him in his crib but not to take him out of it. We had to stand during the entire visit, as the ward was filled with crib patients, and visiting hours produced a set of parents for each one. Strangers in white did for Elliot the services rightfully ours to perform.

Now we were taking him home. He was ours again. We rebelled against the tough policy which the doctor directed. Everything inside of us cried out for a chance to shelter him, to keep the evil world out. Hadn't he had enough? At nine months, he had walked around furniture but now, at a year, he could not support himself on those same legs. His right arm was completely limp, and the shoulder muscle was rated as zero. Must we let him make his own way in the world right away?

This business of keeping our sympathy and our common sense separated remained a struggle. But we knew the doctor was right. And having a baby every two years made it more natural to let him grow up without being overindulged.

In time, Elliot did everything little boys do, but he learned a little later. Shortly after his homecoming, he raced his walker all over the house; from walking on his own two feet, he took up running, often coming up bloody. Many times I watched him as he ran out to meet his daddy, tension gripping me as I waited for the inevitable fall. The joyous face, accompanied by shrieks of "Hi, Daddy! Hi, Daddy!" as he ran with his right arm dangling like a rag, would be succeeded by Daddy's running to pick up a broken-hearted little boy, bleeding again in the lip.

Elliot completely bypassed the climbing phase, inasmuch as he didn't have two arms with which to pull himself up. I never had to worry about stairs. By the time he was mobile, his judgment warned him of danger.

As he grew up we diligently avoided excessive solicitude. Many times, with hearts in our throats, we watched him attempt some new feat. I aged years the day I looked on as he climbed the monkey bars at the park—his right arm limp at his side; his left letting go of each bar in order to reach for a higher one while he hung suspended in space.

When we asked him to do a chore for us, we gave him no more assistance than necessary. When he took the garbage out to the can, he had to lay it down by the door, open the door, pick up the garbage, lay it down outside the door, close the door, pick up the garbage, walk to the garbage can, lay down the garbage, open the can, place the garbage in it, and close the can. We ached to help him, but common sense told us to heed the doctor's warning. Elliot would have no one going before him all his life opening doors.

His serene personality did not rebel against his lot. Every day he taught us a lesson in patience. When he was three or four his theme, "I love everybody in the whole world," revealed his healthy mental attitude. His determination commanded our honest admiration and touched our hearts.

We did not try to conceal our emotion the day he first put his left knee in a coaster wagon, his left hand on the handle, and slowly coasted down the walk, his right arm hanging limp, fingers resting on the side of the wagon. He learned to roller-skate and to ride a tricycle and then a bike. He played all kinds of ball and could use a catcher's mitt. He developed a perfect rhythm of wearing the mitt to catch, throwing it into his right hand to return the ball, putting it back on his left hand to receive the next ball.

One day, when Elliot was four and a half, he burst

into the house, breathless from putting distance between himself and pursuers who were shouting something I could not hear. His face was flushed from the heat of summer. My world dropped as I sensed that there was a new problem.

"Mommy, those boys are calling me 'Skinny Arm,' " he sobbed, hope and despair coming together in the soft eyes that were naturally serene and peaceful.

Kneeling beside him on the floor, my first reaction was: "I really flubbed. I should have kept long sleeves on him all the time." But once again, I remembered the warning the doctor had given us at the time he was discharged from the hospital: "Don't consider him 'the boy with the arm.' " A sleeve over his thin, limp arm would only conceal the handicap, causing it to become a thing of shame. I had to teach him to live with it, bearing it with dignity.

As his troubled face searched mine, I prayed for wisdom.

"Elliot," I began, "there's something you must try to understand. Let's look at your arms." I held them both up. "Look how nice and fat this arm is," I said. "See, it has a dimple in the elbow—and look, it stays up by itself."

Elliot became quite interested. "Now let's look at this one. See, it drops when I let it go, and it hangs straight down, doesn't it? The muscles are not used, so the arm is very thin. This is because you had polio when you were a baby. You know this, don't you?" He nodded. "So, you see, your right arm *is* really a skinny arm, just as they say, isn't it?" He nodded his head reluctantly.

"Your friends don't know *why* it's skinny," I continued. "They just see that it's different from your other arm. They really like you, Elliot. You shouldn't mind too much if they say 'Skinny Arm.' "

"But Mommy, I *do* mind," he said, a large tear dropping from his black eyelashes, his mouth quivering again.

Taking a deep breath, I realized mere logic would not persuade him that his peers were engaged in harmless sport.

"Elliot, we know that what they say is true, and we know we can't make them stop saying it. So let's try to make you so you won't mind it."

"Huh? What?" he asked.

"Elliot, I'm going to call you 'Skinny Arm' part of the time. Maybe Daddy will, too. Perhaps if *we* call you that, it won't bother you to have others do it."

He gave me an incredulous look, with a weak smile.

I had several opportunities to call him by the despised name in the next few days. At first I did it jokingly when our fun was at its highest pitch; then I cushioned it with tenderness as though it were the sweetest name a mother could give her child. After giving it every possible connotation, I teased him with it. At first he noticed it, but he took it good-naturedly. And finally he ignored it.

Elliot is now thirty years old. He has come up against many problems, but has met them with admirable poise. As far as I can determine, he was never again persecuted for his handicap. I have a hunch the self-confidence that grew out of the skinny-arm incident gave him a bearing that assured any would-be tormentors that Elliot was no mere cripple, but he was every inch a man.

Correct Prayer

I rushed through my work. Andrew was coming in forty-five minutes. Our only grandchild, Andy, two and a half, is always the man of the house when he comes.

Grace had a dental appointment after which she and her family were to have dinner with us. I had stuffed a turkey and made a pie. I hurried to scrub the potatoes and fill a relish dish, for after Andy's arrival, I'd want to play the record player with him. Clint had just bought a new needle for the old three-speed we had given our children over twenty years ago.

Larry, our son-in-law, brought Andy and left. Andy caught on to the procedure of the phonograph and enjoyed the mechanics of it so much he hardly had time to listen to the scratched and noisy records.

After lunch we did one of our favorite things together—we went for a bus ride to St. Paul. This poor disadvantaged child gets to ride only in Oldsmobiles and "blazers" when he's at home; if he is ever to ride a bus, I have to take him. He loves to "cross the river," and see the superette with a gas station whose sign has a car on it that "goes round and round." A little farther along, we see the "beautiful basilica" with the green roof. Then we go down a steep hill, but from its height we can already view "the big round Civic Center." In downtown St. Paul we scan the rooftops until once more we see the "big gold bird on the roof" of a bank. When we first started these trips, Andrew knew only that dogs say "Ruff," so whenever he would tell someone about the big gold bird on the bank he would say "on the roof!" and sound like a St. Bernard.

We were returning from St. Paul and Andy had fallen asleep, which is what usually happens on one of these trips, when I remembered Grace's appointment with the dentist. Grace had feared the dentist ever since childhood and, out of fear, had postponed going until her teeth were in very bad shape. She has such beautiful teeth, her smile being her loveliest feature, we were all hoping the fillings would stick and no abscesses would form. Now I prayed, "And, Lord, please don't let Grace be hurt as badly as the last time. Just be with her, Lord."

When Andy woke up, he found himself, as usual on these occasions, in a cart in the superette where I'd promised to stop and buy him a treat. "The bus!" he exclaimed in disappointment. We bought pink peppermints and walked home at his speed. He climbed the banks of snow in more than one yard, stopping frequently to watch squirrels romping in the trees. I was colder than he, it seemed, and occasionally had to resort to games to get him on the move again. "Bet you can't catch me." When he became discouraged, I'd let him catch me. Then it would be his turn. "Bet you can't catch me," he'd cry, and his little legs, heavily bound in a red snowmobile suit and weighted with white boots, moved as fast as they could.

When we arrived home at 1:45, Andy's cheeks were red as winesaps and his eyes as blue as the sky. I thought again of Grace's 3:30 appointment. "Andy," I said, "let's pray for your mommy, shall we?" Andy loves to fold his hands and pray. Not wanting to alarm him with terminology about the dentist, I just said, "Dear Jesus, please take care of Mommy. Help her to feel better. And help her to come here happy tonight."

As Andy joined me in the "Amen," I thought, it is a good thing God knows exactly what our needs are, even when expressed in two-year-old terms.

Grace and Larry were due at 5:00. They arrived a little early and Grace said, "You know, I went back to bed after Larry brought Andy over here because I haven't been getting enough sleep. And I never did get to the dentist."

I thought, "That's strange. Why did God lead me to pray as he did?"

"About noon," Grace was saying, "I woke up feeling so sick, so nauseated. An hour later I called the dentist and canceled my appointment. The thought of it—his fingers in my mouth—" and she shuddered. Yet, here she was, obviously hungry, sampling chunks of turkey off the platter even as I carved the bird.

Andy and I had been on our ride from 12:00 until about 1:45 and I had prayed twice. Now I knew how appropriate my words had been. Here was Grace, "feeling better" and "happy."

Bus Ride

Andy and I were on one of our bus rides to St. Paul. Andy is more of a people-watcher than a sightseer, and I watched him as he observed persons of all types mounting the steps, paying their fares, and finding seats. Sleepily, Andy's eyes followed each one. I wished I knew what he was thinking. He lives in white suburbia. This ride was taking us through one of the lowest-income areas in the Twin Cities, inhabited by minorities and poor whites. Here ride the toothless, the obese, the intoxicated, and the thinly clad.

The door opened and a black woman came on with a little boy Andy's age. She paid her fare, scanned the busload with an expression somewhere between a scowl and a frown, and sat herself down on one of the long seats along the side at the front of the bus, right next to our seats which faced forward. She pulled her little one up next to her and handed him a bag of cheese-flavored popcorn. She opened it for him, then opened the can of soda pop she had in her hand and put the opening of the can to the boy's lips. She then put it to her own, and the boy put his fingers into his bag.

The fingers had made a few trips from the bag to his mouth and were greasy by the time the woman, whose glance had included Andy and me several times, poked the boy and said, "Give *him* some," indicating Andy, who looked more sleepy than hungry.

Obediently, the boy slipped his wet fingers back into the bag and pulled out a morsel of popcorn, which he handed to Andy. I don't know what prevented Andy from accepting it, but I was embarrassed that this overture was rejected; so I took it from the boy, thanked him, and offered it to Andy, who then took it from me.

I tried to meet the woman's eyes, but her glances never gave me the opportunity to smile. A few minutes later, she commanded the boy again, "Give *him* some," and the boy willingly offered, on slippery fingers, another tidbit, which Andy now accepted willingly.

Behind this little incident I see a lesson—of sharing what you have that your brother lacks; of receiving from someone who may have less than you; of accepting little overtures of love and friendship between the races, between the haves and the have-nots; and I see it isn't always the whites who have and the blacks who have not.

I see the urgency of overcoming our antipathy for other types of people. Andy may have been reluctant to accept that gift, but I'm quite sure his reticence was not because the fingers that offered it were wet, nor because they were black. More likely, he was shy. And I see that sometimes it takes a go-between, as I had been.

I think I'll long remember that mother poking her son and saying matter-of-factly: "Give *him* some."

Lord, we don't have to have much to share. Help us all to work at bridging gaps between races and peoples as unpatronizingly as this woman and child did, and to reciprocate as gratefully as Andy and I did. Amen.

The Test

 "Bill Rikkers is in the hospital," I said to Clint on our way home from church one Sunday.

"What for; do you know?"

"No. I think I'll go see him this week."

As I drove I-94 from Minneapolis to St. Paul a few days later, I reminisced about the Rikkers family. Bill's parents had served the church Clint and I belonged to right after World War II. Rev. Rikkers had baptized our first three children. Mrs. Rikkers' insights into Scripture had inspired me weekly at the ladies' Bible fellowship. Now Bill's father lay buried by the sea in California where Mrs. Rikkers still lived and worked in a retirement home.

Bill had married his high school sweetheart, Marge Olson, and they chose for their family the same church we had joined in 1955, First Covenant of Minneapolis.

Because we knew and loved his parents, we took Bill and Marge and their children to our hearts and, perhaps because his parents had loved us, Bill and Marge took us to theirs.

I had no idea what Bill was in the hospital for. Recently two of his brothers had had heart attacks and his father had been a heart patient the last decade of his life.

I parked the car and found Bill. He seemed delighted to see me. "We can stay right here," he said, indicating a little waiting room, empty until we entered it.

"Well, what's your problem, Bill? You look OK to me."

He flashed his usual smile which always had a hint of shyness in it. How much he looks like his mother, I thought. Same strong jaw. His eyes brighter than hers—maybe more like his father's.

"Last Friday," Bill said, "I felt some tightness and discomfort in my chest and I called the doctor. Because of our family's history of heart problems, he put me in the hospital over the weekend for observation, but no problems developed.

"Well, I was feeling better and was looking forward to going home on Monday. But then, when my doctor came in on Monday, he told me that the X-ray—they give everyone a routine X-ray upon admittance—had disclosed a spot on the right lung and that further tests would be required."

I didn't interrupt him. He had seemed quite calm when he started but now his hands were clenched in his lap.

"Well, additional tests that afternoon confirmed the existence of a spot a little smaller than a dime." Bill's eyes flashed a quick glance at mine, as if to catch my reaction before I could control it.

I didn't say anything but was thinking, "Just like my brother Jack. Cancer. It starts with a little spot. A harmless-looking little spot."

Bill continued. "The doctors have recommended surgery." His voice had grown tight and husky. He didn't need to tell me about his fears of death, and of his thoughts about his wife and three children under twelve.

"Have you told your mother?"

"Not yet. I'm planning to call her tonight. Yesterday when they confirmed the spot, and the reality of this thing sunk in—well, I was pretty shocked. And really, Ruth, Mother has gone through so much this past year. Bob and Rich both had heart attacks and she was pretty depressed over that. I really didn't know how I was going to tell her about this." The emotion was beginning to show in Bill's face.

"You know, Ruth, on my visits to Santa Barbara to see Mother, I've become acquainted with her pastor, Bryan Leech, of the Monticeto Covenant Church.

Well, last night I was worrying about telling Mother about this development and I started to think about Bryan Leech. I got the idea to call him and ask him to explain my situation to Mother before I would call her."

Bill continued, "I called him, and after explaining the situation to him, he said that he would be happy to talk to Mother. He then told me something amazing, Ruth. You just can't imagine—you just wouldn't believe—" Bill was now fighting to control his emotions. "As I had been telling him about the spot on my lung, he'd been remembering something. He said that he had been trying to get the members of his church to become more involved in a loving way in each other's lives, to pray for each other and support each other in meeting the daily problems with which we're all faced. Each member was to draw the name of another member and then try to show the love of Christ in a special way, and to pray especially for the needs of that member. He said that 'quite by chance' he had drawn the name of my mother."

Tears had begun to course down Bill's cheeks. He got up and closed the door. Struggling, he continued. "He said that he had been praying not only for her, but *also for the needs of her children.*"

I was weeping too, but Bill wasn't finished. "Bryan and I talked for a few more minutes, and just before saying good-bye, I asked him to remember me in his prayers. He responded very simply, 'I already have.' "

We sat in sacred silence as the impact, that had struck Bill with such force at the time, reached me. Bill said, "Before I even knew I had a special need, God had moved through circumstances 2000 miles away, and a very special person had been praying for me. Neither he nor I even knew of the existence or nature of that special need at the time."

We sat in silence, thinking, weeping, and praising.

The next day Bill called me at home. "They've scheduled surgery for next week, but before I leave the hospital they are going to give me several skin tests which they want to check prior to going ahead with the surgery."

A jubilant Bill telephoned me a few days later from home. "I had a positive reaction to one of the tests, and they suspect that the spot on my lung may be histoplasmosis, which is a type of fungus. They're going to delay the surgery and look at the spot again in three months. They think it may disappear."

"Oh, Bill, wouldn't that be wonderful?" It seemed like a reprieve from a death sentence.

Three months later Bill telephoned to let me know that the spot was smaller. Within six months it had become a calcified speck.

One might wonder about God's purpose in all of this. Without that X-ray, Bill would have never known he had that spot on his lung. One might ask, "Did he and Marge need to endure that anxiety in order to deal with the question of death?" Or did God want to show them how he goes ahead of them and provides for every need? As he says in Isaiah 65:24, "Before they call, I will answer."

Surely the Lord's ways are past finding out, but Bill's faith was renewed and deepened as a result of this experience.

O Lord, Thou hast searched me and known me. Thou dost know when I sit down and when I rise up; Thou dost understand my thought from afar. Thou dost scrutinize my path and my lying down, and art intimately ac-

quainted with all my ways. Even before there is a word on my tongue, behold, O Lord, Thou dost know it all. Thou hast enclosed me behind and before, and laid Thy hand upon me. Such knowledge is too wonderful for me. Amen.

The Stain

Mother had new shoes. She seldom bought anything for herself in those days of hard times on the farm. We had to sell our cream and eggs to buy flour and yeast. There were times when we had no butter on our bread. On Easter we were permitted to have all the eggs we wanted, which, under normal conditions, would have been no big treat for farm children.

Mother sewed as many of our clothes as she could. She once made me a dress of pink organdy that cost nine cents a yard. Even at that price, she had skimped in buying and ended up with not quite enough. The dress was much too tight, but I had to wear it anyway. I even managed to wear it through one extra summer before the seams split.

Grandma lived with us winters and did the mending. By patching holes in patches on underwear and overalls, Grandma extended the lives of these expensive garments. I think Grandma may have supplied the money for Mother's new shoes. I can't imagine where else she could have found the $1.67 to order them from Montgomery Ward's. They were lovely —gray kid and dainty pointed toes. A narrow band, decorated with a tiny silvery button, ran across each shoe at the instep.

I wouldn't remember these shoes if tragedy hadn't struck one Sunday. I was eight. We had been to an afternoon church service and Mother had worn her new shoes for the first time. We returned to a cold house; the fire in our little black heater had gone out. Mother moved fast. With her hat and coat still on, she laid on a few sticks, crumpled a sheet of *Grit,* and doused it all with kerosene. *Pfuff*—out flew the flames. No, it wasn't the flames that formed the tragedy. It was the kerosene.

I was merely an observer, a bystander. I felt no grief. But today it brings tears to my eyes when I think of that afternoon. The winter sun was going down. Dad came in from the garage. We all were standing around, waiting for the little potbellied stove, which Mother always kept highly polished, to throw off some heat. Then Mother spied the oil on her shoe. She didn't cry out or wail. She stared at it in disbelief. Then she shook her head from side to side slowly and made a little smack with her lips. We all stood in silence, our eyes fixed on that stain. How would she react to this calamity? I looked from the shoe to her face and back to her shoe. Finally, she spoke. "I must have loved them too much. It'll never come out. It's there for good."

And it was. Efforts to remove that stain only made it spread. She wore those shoes every Sunday for several years, the spot a painful reminder of her "worldliness."

When I tend to get too attached to material things, I remember Mother's gray kid slippers.

Stop loving this evil world and all that it offers you . . . This world is fading away, and these evil, forbidden things will go with it, but whoever keeps doing the will of God will live forever (1 John 2:15, 17, TLB).

Lord, I'm so grateful for lessons Mother taught me. She so seldom got anything new, yet she didn't question or grumble when that oil spot dampened her joy in wearing those shoes. Help me, too, to learn what you're trying to teach me, and to accept your will for my life, as Mother did for hers. Amen.

Reservation

We were planning another trip to California. Last year, we had gone to see our son Elliot and to meet his fiancée. We also visited our daughter Grace and her husband and welcomed into the world our first grandchild. This year, we were going to Elliot's and Cheryl's wedding.

Clint liked having motel reservations. None of this hunting for a place to sleep after a long day's journey for him. He spent hours locating motels along the way, spaced so that we could make the trip in three to four days. He would telephone each motel for a reservation and send his check if they required a deposit. In some cases he received an acknowledgment showing they had made a reservation in his name.

Nevertheless, if we spent more time sightseeing, or if we were delayed by car trouble, or if the trip surprised us with added miles, he would still feel uncertain about it. "Check the folder again and see if there's a card from Best Western confirming our reservation," he would say. Even though he had asked them to hold it for late arrival, he never felt positive that a room would be kept for us. How relieved we would be to find our room waiting, held by our reservation.

Then one day our pastor, David L. Larsen, First Covenant Church, Minneapolis, preached on Colossians 1:9-18, "Partakers of the Inheritance." I especially remember the second point of that message: "This inheritance is something prospective." He said, "There is a great aspect of this inheritance which is future, which awaits us in glory, into which not *all* of the *aeons* of eternity itself, the *endless reaches* of eternity will be able to fully initiate us. We are going to spend *all* eternity exploring and experiencing the inheritance of the saints in light.

"The Holy Spirit—that precious gift—is the earnest of this *full* inheritance—the indication and evidence—the foretaste of the redemption of the promised or purchased possession."

In his animation, his hands and arms were never still. On "all" and "full," he made a huge expansive circle with his arms. On the words, "endless reaches of eternity," he thrust his arms out in front of him, indicating a seemingly endless tunnel.

Lowering his voice and smiling tenderly, he said, "The Holy Spirit is like the engagement ring. Oh," his face brightened, "what a delight that engagement ring is! What a joy! But it's just the sign of something

83

that is yet to come that is even better and more glorious." His brown eyes were sparkling in his ruddy, unlined face.

"We have been promised 'an eternal inheritance,' Hebrews 9:15. We are the 'heirs of the kingdom of God,' James 2:5. Oh, there's something ahead!" He swung around to address the choir. "There's something awaiting the believer. That inheritance is described by Peter as 'incorruptible, undefiled, that fades not away.'"

He turned back to the congregation. "How many have looked forward to an inheritance upon this earth and have been disappointed. How many people have seen what they thought was to be their inheritance slip from their grasp and be gone. But this inheritance for the believer is incorruptible—death cannot destroy it. It is undefiled—sin cannot destroy it. It fadeth not away—not all natural powers in the universe can destroy it. Moth and rust cannot corrupt it. Thieves cannot break through to steal it. Our eyes with all they have seen, and our ears with all they have heard, and our hands with all their activity have not begun to grasp or encompass the things which the Lord prepared for those who love him in this life and in the life to come." His joyous voice resounded in the auditorium like a sustained chord.

He continued, "The Spirit shows us this inheritance incorruptible, undefiled, that fades not away. It's reserved in heaven for us. Oh, I am so grateful the Lord has made a reservation for me up there. It's so wonderful to have a reservation, but here on earth you can't always count on it. Sometimes there's a slipup."

Yes, there sometimes is. My mind returned to the Decision School of Christian Writing. My editor had apologized for not having heard me speak earlier in the morning. "I was bumped from my plane and didn't reach my hotel room until three this morning," he explained.

Pastor Larsen was now saying, "But, my friends, there's going to be no slipup." His eyebrows arched over a serious face. "That reservation has been made and it is sealed through our Lord Jesus Christ, and this inheritance is being reserved in heaven for us."

How wonderful! My soul was soaring.

"It's held on deposit! Praise God for that! It is in our name, through Jesus Christ, up in heaven. All that he has promised us he is holding for us, reserved in heaven for us."

I didn't even need the rest of that sermon. His third point was dessert to a soul that was full.

Prayer Pact

We'd just completed the eight weeks of my Beginners' Writing Course in one of the Minneapolis schools. The next quarter's classes were about to begin, so I telephoned a few of my former students to see if they were planning to take the advanced course for the next eight weeks. One of them, a woman near my own age, explained why she couldn't.

"I didn't tell you this, but my home's breaking up. One reason I didn't do all your assignments was because I just felt too bad. My husband drinks and he goes around with men who drink and are divorced. He's been so critical of everything I do, and now—" She couldn't finish.

I tried to comfort her.

She continued. "I took your course because I had to do something to keep my sanity. I couldn't do anything right at home. I love him—." Tears took over completely. She couldn't talk, and I was having trouble talking, but I had to offer Jesus' help. "Why don't you turn the whole matter over to God? Try to trust him completely for the outcome. We know it's his will that husband and wife live together in love. Keep yourself open to God and do whatever he tells you to." We formed a prayer pact, claiming Matthew 18:19: ". . . if two of you agree down here on earth concerning anything you ask for, my Father in heaven will do it for you" (TLB).

She promised to pray for God's will in her marriage and do what he led her to do. "I started going to church again. I was so desperate. Yes, I'm finding comfort there."

When I hung up that day, I prayed for this woman as if I'd known her all my life. For the moment she was my sister. I recalled her behavior in class the preceding weeks. She had always come a bit early. One night, she drove up to the school just as I did, greeting me with a cheery, "I baked a cake!" We had a party at break that night. I remembered her gentle face, the sweetness of her smile. She wrote about her father who was a hobo. He would show up once or twice a year. Her mother had moved the family in with her parents, and my student recalled that her grandmother hated her father. I had one problem with this student. She talked too much in class. Sometimes I ran out of ways to continue my lecture without offending her. I understand now that it was nervousness which made her so talkative.

After talking with her that day, the Holy Spirit often brought her face before me. I prayed that the Lord's will would be done in that marriage and in the hearts of my friend and her husband. Months went by. I didn't call her or hear from her.

A year later, when I sent a form letter to many of my former students, I thought of each of them as I addressed the envelopes. This caused me to close my letter by saying, "I often smile at the humorous, and reflect on the serious articles each of you read in class and wonder if you ever sold them." Some had written personal experiences of tragedy and sorrow. We came to know each other through sharing. I wrote, "I often flash prayers your way."

This letter spurred a telephone call from my new friend. "I got my husband back. He's joined Alcoholics Anonymous and has stayed off drink for six months. We've turned back to God, too," she said. After my exclamations of joy, I told her I had been faithful in praying for them. Then I felt I wanted to say one thing more.

I realized this student-teacher relationship might never be resumed. I can't keep in close touch with the hundreds of people the Lord brings into my life through my classes. So I had to find out what she meant by "turning back to God."

She explained, "At AA they call it a Higher Power. My husband and I both believe in God. We know this is an answer to prayer and we have really turned back to him."

Not quite satisfied with this, I pressed, "And do you know Christ? The Bible says he is the only door to God."

She answered, "Yes. But we're not back in church yet. We plan to start, though. I went by myself for awhile, but—"

I had to leave it like that for the moment, but I just might call her again sometime.

Angie

She greeted me at her door with, "I have something for you." Her eyes avoided mine. "I'm told these plates are antiques. They're called 'Tree of Life.' " She unwrapped them from their tissue paper—two leaf-shaped salad plates of clear glass on which were etched the branches of a tree. She repeated, "I'm told they're worth quite a bit—I don't know—but I wanted you to have them."

"Oh, Angie, how lovely! I'll really treasure these." I looked from the plates into her eyes.

She looked away with an embarrassed, fleeting smile. An attractive woman in her mid-fifties, Angie had a lovely smile.

I kissed her cheek. "I'll leave them to my two daughters," I said, "with a note that they're from my friend Angie Kraft Ries, formerly from Strasburg. Grace has met you and will remember you."

She nodded. Angie's pride in Strasburg and the folks from North Dakota always surprised me. Her heart had never really left there. She could tell you the accomplishments of many graduates from that high school.

We both knew why she had given me these plates. Her cancer had returned, and Angie was a very practical person. We were to grow very close the last six months of her life.

She and her husband had moved to Bloomington, Minnesota, and she had seen my name in a bulletin from Normandale Community College. She had called me, and we had renewed a friendship which began when we were childhood playmates in Strasburg. She enriched my life the next two-and-a-half years. We talked freely about our faith, so precious to us both. I couldn't outgive Angie. Even during her last weeks at home, I would always carry back in my shopping bag as much as I had carried to her. Whatever she brought back from Strasburg she shared with me, including kuchen and pickles.

When I would drive home to North Dakota to visit Mother, Angie would go with me to see her parents. She made a good traveling companion. Sometimes we'd sing the songs of our high school glee club: "Drink to Me Only with Thine Eyes," and "Believe Me If All Those Endearing Young Charms." We would discuss theology and politics, and talk intimately of ourselves and our families. No one was prouder of my meager accomplishments than Angie, partly, I think, because I had my origin in Strasburg.

Chemotherapy caused Angie's hair to fall out and her feet to swell. If I arrived a bit early, she would hobble to the bathroom as fast as she could to put on her wig and cover her thin hair.

She never gave up hope of recovering. The last time I visited her in her apartment, she asked me to mend some clothes for her, fully intending to wear them again. But there were times when she was discouraged. "My platelets are still down," she would

89

report. She could name every drug she was getting and any possible alternatives. Sometimes she thought the doctors had neglected her and now it was too late. Then she would talk about death and her eyes showed anger and pain. In the next breath she would talk about taking a trip. "I'd go by air, but I don't think I could get out if there were an emergency," she said, viewing her thick feet. I marveled that one dying of cancer could worry about an airplane crash.

Clint and I biked to the university hospital several times the last three weeks of her life. I talked to her by phone the morning of the day she died. Her sister, Sister Catherine, told me Angie was very sleepy, that she would be able to hear me but not talk. I thought it was strange that she had declined so rapidly in two days. I told Angie, "I'll be going to see Mother next week, and I'll be thinking of you because of all the good trips to Strasburg you and I made together. Only this time, I'll be going east instead of west. Mother's in Wisconsin now."

Little grunts told me she understood me, but soon the phone was taken again by her sister.

I felt I had to see Angie again before leaving for Wisconsin, and decided I would go after church the following day. There were things I wanted to say to her once more. I wanted to put my hand on her forehead and tell her how dear she was to me. I wanted to whisper right into her ear, "Angie, I've never had such a dear friend as you—one who loved me the way you do." She had held me close and shared herself with me. Her esteem for me reflected back, increasing my sense of self-worth.

John Powell, in "Why Am I Afraid to Love?" says: "The image each of us has of himself is really the product of what other people, rightly or wrongly, have told us that we are. . . . We desperately need to see in the mirror of another's eyes our own goodness and beauty if we are to be truly free." This gift Angie gave me, and I hope I also gave it to her.

Angie died that night at 9:20. My pain of regret for having missed the opportunity to tell her these things again is eased by her own words the last time I was with her. On that occasion Angie's husband, mother and sister Isabel had joined us in the hospital room after they returned from supper. Upon seeing Isabel, whom I hadn't seen since she and my brother John graduated from high school in 1938, I exclaimed, "What a pretty lady you are!" Later I said again, "I wish I could tell John how pretty you are!" John had died in 1971.

From the bed came these words: "He knows."

We all turned in astonishment. She repeated, through white lips, "He knows. Don't you think he knows?"

She had come to share my own belief. Many times Angie and I had talked of heaven. Shortly after my father's death in 1973, several good things had happened to me. I felt my father knew about all of them. Angie and I had agreed that surely Dad had more knowledge now than he had while he was with us.

Yes, I believe Jack knows. And it comforts me to believe Angie knows how dear I will always hold her in my heart.

The "tree of life" plates remind me that Angie has entered into eternal life. Enjoy, Beloved Friend.

Light

According to the Bible, you and I are lights. Our light doesn't depend on how we feel. We can't make ourselves become lights. No one else can make us lights.

We are lights because God has declared us lights as a result of our association with Christ the true Light "which lighteth every man" (John 1:9). As the moon has no light of its own, but reflects the light of the sun, so we have no light except as we reflect the light of Christ.

After Moses had spent forty days and nights on Mt. Sinai with God, his face had such a shine that the people were awed. Yet we read, "Moses [knew] not that the skin of his face shone" (Exodus 34:29).

In the same way, if you are Christ's, you are a light whether you feel like one or not. God *says* you are a light, and the world *knows* you are one.

In the days of the plagues upon Egypt, God showed special favor to his people, the Israelites. When the Egyptians suffered disease, natural disasters, and death, the Israelites enjoyed health, calm, and life. When the Egyptians were cast into darkness so deep it could be felt, the Israelites had light in their dwellings (Exodus 10:23).

The Egyptians must have seen the lights in the windows of the Israelites over in Goshen. They must have longed for light, but they didn't dare move out of their places, so dark was their darkness.

The world's darkness is still such that those living in it cannot move toward us out of their darkness. We have to move toward them. We may be tempted to stay in our light dwellings and warm ourselves by the fires of Christian love, but out there in the darkness, men, women, and children are perishing because of their sin. We must force ourselves out of our homes and into the darkness. We needn't fear that the world won't see our light. A lit match will be obvious in a dark cathedral. Any uncovered light will be seen. It doesn't have to go around saying, "I'm a light. Let me help you in your darkness." No, those in darkness will automatically turn to the light.

When we forget and behave like those in darkness, the world is disappointed. It expects certain standards from its light-bearers.

Father, help me show the characteristics of light when I move about in the darkness of the world around me. Grant that others may see your light shining through me and glorify your name. Amen.

Blanche

I'd like you to meet Blanche. At first she was named Sophie—Sophie Lillian. Her mother was a domestic in Oakes, North Dakota. When the farm folks for whom she worked learned their son had become involved with the hired girl, they quietly sent him to Colorado. The girl continued to work for them until the time came for her baby to be born. Then they took her to a hospital in Oakes. Two weeks later, this twenty-four-year-old mother was taken to Fargo, where she surrendered her little girl for adoption.

When Sophie was three weeks old, a childless couple named Wagner chose her out of the orphanage. Joyfully, they brought home their baby, renaming her "Blanche." After living in Fargo for a year, the family moved to Minneapolis.

I met Blanche in 1955 when we joined First Covenant Church. By then a beautiful woman of middle age, Blanche was the church librarian. At the midweek prayer meeting, I soon observed that here was a unique individual. She prayed most knowledgeably and specifically for the missionaries. I learned that Blanche, who had never married, worked for Northwest Airlines and used her privilege of reduced air fare to visit the many missionaries sponsored by the church. When our semiannual missionary conferences occurred, Blanche would set up showcases, artistically displaying her souvenirs from all over the world.

For twenty-two years, Blanche chaperoned the children on the Sunday school bus, which meant she rose early in the morning and rode the bus for an hour before Sunday school. Then Blanche rode the bus again after church as the children were delivered back to their homes.

I came to love this pleasant little woman who had a tendency to roundness. She moved about with purpose in every step, her large, lively eyes ever glancing about for someone to greet. She would cross the foyer to tell me of a missionary who needed prayer or a special speaker I should be sure to hear.

In 1962 Blanche suffered paralysis of one cord of her larynx, which forced her to give up singing in the church choir. She regained full use of her voice but, upon her doctor's advice, didn't resume singing.

About that time, she began to take a great interest

in the services for the deaf who worshiped in our sanctuary through the use of an interpreter. Blanche joined them and soon learned enough sign language to become good friends with them. A year later, when their leader left, Blanche took over the work of interpreting the service, which she did for two years. Her friendship with the deaf continues today as she is one of the few who has made the effort to communicate with them.

In 1966 Blanche finally gave up her long-entertained hope of one day being a foreign missionary. Her education as a child had been interrupted several times by family moves. By 1932, when she was baptized and joined First Covenant Church, she began to feel the call to be a missionary. Obediently, she finished her high school by correspondence and started going to Northwestern College at night. Later, she also took courses at St. Paul Bible Institute. She came within nine credits of graduation.

But her dream was not to be fulfilled. In 1947 her adoptive mother became ill with heart trouble and needed Blanche's care. Mr. Wagner was an alcoholic. He had been led to the Lord in 1934 by Pastor Gilbert Otteson, but had not been able to conquer his craving for alcohol, and this seriously blighted the home.

Mrs. Wagner lived until 1954. On her deathbed she assured Blanche that she was going to be with the Lord. Two years later, Blanche's father died. When his death became imminent, Blanche questioned him about his salvation. He said his trust was in Christ.

It was now 1956 and Blanche was almost fifty years old. She had exhausted herself caring for her parents while continuing to work for Northwest. But she still held to the hope of being a foreign missionary. Then in 1966 she had a heart attack, and her dream was ended.

But Blanche had always been a missionary—a home missionary in the best sense of the word. Her parents and her younger sister Kay were saved as a result of Blanche becoming a Christian and joining First Covenant Church.

At twelve years of age, Blanche had desired a New Testament and received one as a gift. She read it faithfully without really understanding it. Some of it got through to her, however, and prepared her for the deeper work of the Holy Spirit.

After going to many different churches, Blanche started at our church, which was then called the Swedish Tabernacle. She says, "I had a wonderful Sunday school teacher. She's the one who prayed me into the kingdom of God. But she must have had many times of heartbreak, for I was worldly for a long time. But then one day the Lord truly came in, and I found a joy that helped me through many hard years."

Besides her family, Blanche has led a good number of friends to God, and has witnessed to hundreds of others. A few years ago, I was with her when she was to have gall bladder surgery. She witnessed to the young man who wheeled her into the operating room. Though I left her at the door, I'm quite sure she told a few more attendants about her Savior before she surrendered to the anesthesia. Joy exudes from her like a heady fragrance.

In 1972 Blanche rode with me to a writing class held at beautiful Lake Minnetonka. As we drove, she would point out the name of nearly every tame and wild flower, every vine, and every growing thing. After we had reached our destination, and as we were walking to the door of the YWCA, she would frequently drop to one knee to take a picture of a bed of violets, or of lichen on a tree.

In 1974, our church gave a reception for Blanche Wagner. Very few people other than ministers and missionaries have ever had such an honor.

Her health, of late, has been precarious. She is on medication for her heart and for edema, and she chafes under the restrictions placed on her activities. She worships by radio most of the time.

Blanche reads a great deal and also tries her hand at writing. Recently, she wrote: "If I had to live my life over again, would I do as I've done? I've enjoyed life. I've found each day different, and there's been much to see and touch and learn. There have always been horizons which have intrigued and led me on. I've always been interested in others. If there's been a need, I've tried to fill it. The Lord's been good. I've often wondered—what if I'd not been born out of wedlock—or what if I'd not been adopted by my wonderful parents, the Wagners—or *what if I had been conceived in this present day?*" [When so many unwed mothers choose abortion.]

"Each new day is a new adventure—like a spring day or a glowing sunset, the smile of a child, or a 'Hi' from an elderly person," says Blanche. "All of these and time with my Lord each day give me an upward look of thanks for all things. If I had to live my life over again, I believe I'd live it much the same way."

Lord, help us to understand that the child most difficult to bear and rear may be the one you have marked for a special purpose, perhaps of leadership, or of instrumentality in bringing one of your elect into the kingdom. Amen.

Good-bye,
Faith and Hope

Dr. Oswald Hoffman of Lutheran Hour fame was the preacher at a session of the Minnesota Sunday School Convention. Toward the end of his message, he slowly recited 1 Corinthians 13. He refrained from comments until he came to the verse, "Now abideth faith, hope, and love, these three; but the greatest of these is love." Here he explained, in his deep bass voice, "Love is the anchor that holds fast. One day our faith will change into sight. Our hope will change into reality. But our love we'll take with us. It will never change."

Beautiful thought. When I got home, I took my Cruden's Bible Concordance and looked up some of the verses on faith. "But the just shall live by his faith" (Habakkuk 2:4). "Now faith is the substance of things hoped for, the evidence of things not seen" (Hebrews 11:1). "But without faith it is impossible to please him" (Hebrews 11:6). "For by grace are ye saved through faith" (Ephesians 2:8). I read the entire chapter of Hebrews 11, noting that "these all died in faith."

Faith is that great ingredient we need to come to God, to live a righteous life, to die with confidence. No small thing, faith.

And hope. I read in Romans 4:18 that Abraham "against hope believed in hope, that he might become the father of many nations." Romans 5:2 said, "By whom also we have access by faith into this grace wherein we stand, and rejoice in hope of the glory of

God." Romans 5:5: "And hope maketh not ashamed; because the love of God is shed abroad in our hearts by the Holy Ghost which is given unto us." Paul wrote to Titus, "In hope of eternal life, which God, that cannot lie, promised before the world began" (Titus 1:2).

Hope is that celestial fire that keeps faith glowing! Surely hope is also great. But Paul tells us that *love* is even greater than faith and hope.

I had never thought of it before: When I enter heaven's door, I'll have no more need of faith or hope. Faith brought me into the kingdom, and hope sustained me through a lifetime.

Faith took God at his Word when he said I was his child, no matter how far short I came of his plan for me. Faith kept me believing God's promise that the children we trained in the way they should go wouldn't depart from that way when they were old. Faith answered doubt by saying, "Where else will you go, if you turn from God? Jesus alone has eternal life."

Hope often had to reach far down into the valley of despair to lift me up and set me again on the road of faith. Hope kept whispering, "Hold on! Don't give up. There's a crown."

Faith and hope will change when I pass through the gate of heaven. Everything I have believed in faith, I will then see as fact. The crown for over-comers will be mine, but not for long; I will cast it at my Savior's feet. At last, with perfect sight, I will see how great his love for me was for eternity. I will know my own love made perfect.

Beloved, now are we the sons of God, and it doth not yet appear what we shall be: but we know

that, when he shall appear, we shall be like him; for we shall see him as he is (1 John 3:2).

Father, thank you for your gifts of faith and hope which will one day deposit us safely and forever into your haven of love. Amen.

Bessie

Bess and Henry were coming! How I loved to have my only sister and her husband come, even if only for a day. I prepared the best meal I could, estimating it should take about six hours for them to drive from Sheboygan.

There they were. Bess shouted her usual *"Ha-i,"* as soon as she stepped out of the driver's seat. After a hug and kiss, she unlocked the trunk and began to remove the luggage, most of which, it seemed, she planned to carry in herself.

I once read an article about Pat Nixon that reminded me of my dear sister. Brave in sorrow, stoical in suffering, impatient with complainers, cheerful always. But with Bess, it was never forced. Her dimple adds a cute look of mischief to her pretty fair-complexioned face in which her eyes are set like black marbles. When she comes in, cheer wafts in with her.

A half hour later, we were seated at our table enjoying the beef roasted with horseradish. "This is good!" Bess exclaimed. "Isn't this good, Henry?"

"Umm hmmmmmmm!" Henry said. "It *surely* is!"

Clint assured them that everything served at this table was equally good. "I married a good cook!"

100

The four of us reminisced about the times we had gathered up to fifteen at the table for huge dinners in each other's homes.

"Bess," I said, "your cooking was always my model. In fact, *you* were always my model. All my life I wanted to be like you, and for years after I was married, I would say to Clint, 'This is the way Bess does it.'"

She looked so pleased. It made me happy I had told her that. Why had I waited so long?

We were all very hungry, and conversation would have to come later. But after a reflective moment or two, her dimple coming clearly into view, Bess said, altogether without bitterness, "One would never have guessed it from your book, inasmuch as I'm the only family member not even mentioned in it."

"Why, you're right! That's absolutely right! Oh! I never even thought of that before. It never occurred to me—Jack had cancer, and Dad—and Elliot had polio—these—" My cheeks and ears felt as though they'd been squeezed between two hot toasters.

My World Was Too Small had just been published. In it, I had told many stories of my family. Some members were featured in it more than others. I had made a reference to the birth of Bud eight years after me, and the joy it brought our family in 1932. I had passed up a perfect opportunity to mention my only sister when referring to the joy brought into our home by the piano in those desperate years of drought and depression. No one played that piano more than Bess, and it was she who played when we sang together, which was often.

I could have told of the comforting letter she wrote when Elliot was in the Sister Elizabeth Kenny Institute in 1949. She wrote of a mother who had

101

written her soldier son in battle, "I'm building a fortress around you with my prayers," and Bess said this was what she was doing for me. That phrase stayed in my mind and, a quarter of a century later, I used it in my book, *Held for Ransom.*

Four years older than I, Bess had always played with me. When she arrived at her early teens, she was still willing to play paper dolls which we cut out of the mailorder catalogs. We gave them exotic names. We heard about Elliot Roosevelt who lived in the White House, and ever after that, we had a paper doll by that name. I have informed my son we named him after Bess's and my paper doll.

When Bess, as she grew older, required more sophisticated play, she built doll houses for me out of boxes. She papered the walls and made furniture out of matchboxes. We pretended our doll characters were building and furnishing their house. When the house was finished, we played with it some, but it was never as much fun as it had been in the making.

One day, a friend invited me to her house to play with *her* paper dolls. I anticipated a good time. When she brought out Shirley Temple cardboard dolls—children, not even grown-ups—I knew at once I wasn't going to have a good time. They were lifeless, in spite of their extravagant wardrobes. Today, when I find characters in a novel dull and uninteresting I'm reminded of my friend's cardboard dolls. Bess and I had "real" ladies and men and they talked and behaved like adults.

I hadn't answered Bess yet, but I was beginning to realize how I could have overlooked the mention of her. "That says one thing about you, Bess. It says a lot about you—"

Bess looked up.

"It tells me I'm so comfortable in my relationship with you that I felt no pressure—no anxiety—no obligation to include you in the book."

She laughed and seemed assured. I explained a bit more and the matter was dropped.

Now that four years have passed, I still believe that omission came about because with Bess I'm completely at ease. She makes no demands. Her feelings are not easily hurt. In fact, she gave no evidence of hurt feelings when she mentioned the topic.

Dinah Maria Milcock wrote, "Oh, the comfort—the inexpressible comfort of feeling safe with a person, having neither to weigh thoughts nor measure words—but pouring them all right out—just as they are—chaff and grain together—certain that a faithful hand will take and sift them—keep what is worth keeping—and with the breath of kindness blow the rest away."*

Bess is like that. And in that respect, too, I wish I were more like her.

*Copyright © 1936 by Doubleday & Company, Inc. From *The Best Loved Poems of the American People.*

Treasure

The newspaper described it as Edina's biggest residential burglary. Thieves had made off with over a hundred items: furs, guns, ceramics, silver. The loss could not be accurately evaluated, as many of the objects were one of a kind. Heirlooms and collections were stolen along with other appraised valuables.

The family told the police their mother was prostrate with grief. It had taken her and her late husband over thirty years to collect these irreplaceable possessions. A spokesman for the family said, "It's more than a theft; it's a kidnapping. Items in that collection were like children to her. She often touched and caressed them as she walked by the displays."

As my heart went out to this poor woman, I gained insight into Jesus' words, "Lay not up for yourselves treasures upon earth, where moth and rust doth corrupt, and where thieves break through and steal: but lay up for yourselves treasures in heaven, where neither moth nor rust doth corrupt, and where thieves do not break through nor steal" (Matthew 6:19, 20).

Lord, I want to invest my treasure in eternal souls and look forward to the day I will go to where my treasure is. Help me not to love things, but to love only you. Amen.